DURHAM

BIRTH OF A FIRST-CLASS COUNTY

RALPH DELLOR

BLOOMSBURY

First published in Great Britain 1992
Bloomsbury Publishing Limited, 2 Soho Square, London W1V 5DE
in association with Rothmans (UK) Limited

Copyright © 1992 by Ralph Dellor

The moral right of the author has been asserted

A CIP catalogue record for this book
is available from the British Library

ISBN 0 7475 1179 9

Typeset by Hewer Text Composition Services, Edinburgh
Printed by Clays Limited, St Ives plc

Contents

Photo Acknowledgements

Chris Barry/Action-Plus: page 12 *bottom*
Simon Braty/Allsport: page 5
Shaun Botteril/Allsport: page 10 *bottom*
Chris Cole/Allsport: pages 1 *top*, 2–3, 4 *top*, 6–7,
10 *top*, 11 *top*, 16
David Davies/Action-Plus: page 15 *top*
Mike Hewitt/Action-Plus: page 12 *top*
Glyn Kirk/Action-Plus: pages 4 *bottom*, 8, 9, 13,
14 *top* & *bottom*, 15 *bottom*
Adrian Murrell/Allsport: page 11 *bottom*
Don Robson/Durham County Council: page 1 *bottom*

Preface

Shortly before Durham's application for first-class status was considered by the Test and County Cricket Board, I was sent to the county to compile an item on the subject for BBC Television's *Sportsnight* programme. Like most outsiders, I had not fully realised the intensity with which the Durham cricketing fraternity were pursuing their objective. By the time I left the north-east, I was convinced they would achieve their aim of first-class cricket in the region.

After that visit, I followed their progress with more than just a passing interest. I already knew Don Robson from dealings with the National Cricket Association, and Mike Gear was an old friend with whom I had once toured Barbados. Despite the fact that he still owed me at least one rum punch and two wickets from catches he dropped off my bowling, I jumped at the opportunity to write this book when it was offered to me.

It would not have been possible without the help and co-operation of a host of people in the north-east who greeted me with the traditional helpfulness, courtesy and friendliness for which the region is famous. In no particular order, I must extend a special thank you to Ian Caller, Grenville Holland, Don Robson, Mike Gear, Bob Jackson, Tom Moffat, Geoff Cook, David Roberts, Tom Flintoft,

Sam Stoker, Chris Middleton and Tony Brown, and to Brian Hunt, for permission to use his superb statistics; and to all those who regrettably but inevitably must be omitted from a list of this type, my thanks for their time, patience and help.

The rapid rise of Durham County Cricket Club from being a minor county to achieving first-class status will serve as a memorial to all their efforts. I am grateful to have been allowed to witness a remarkable piece of cricket history in the making, and wish the club every possible success in the years to come.

Ralph Dellor
Upper Woolhampton, Berkshire
March, 1992

1

The History of Durham Cricket

The first-class fixtures for the early weeks of the 1992 cricket season contained entries to delight the historian:

14 April   Oxford University v. Durham (Friendly)
19 April   Durham v. Lancashire (Sunday League)
21 April   Durham v. Glamorgan (Benson & Hedges Cup)
25 April   Durham v. Leicestershire (County Championship)

The Durham side scheduled to take the field at The Parks, Oxford, on 14 April would do so as the first to represent the county in a first-class match. Two competitive fixtures at Durham University's Racecourse Ground were quickly to follow, and then that ground was to host the match that had been awaited for 110 years – Durham's entry into the first-class County Championship.

The elevation to first-class status came at the end of a relatively short campaign. The history contained in the previous century and a bit could have – and has – filled volumes in its own right. Even before the official formation of Durham County Cricket Club, in 1882, there was a tradition of good club cricket being played in the county. One of the strongest clubs at the time was South Shields, and it was to this club that much of the credit for the formation of a county club went.

On Wednesday 10 May 1882 the South Shields committee met at what is now called the County Hotel but was then known as the Westoe Tavern. Among the items on the agenda was the subject of county matches. Long discussions ensued, but it was finally decided to appoint a subcommittee to contact other clubs in the county. They were each asked to send their honorary secretary to a meeting at the Three Tuns Hotel, Durham, on Tuesday 23 May. At eight o'clock that evening they would be asked 'to consider the desirability of forming a County Committee for the arranging and selecting of teams to play in County matches'.

It says something for the efficiency of communications in 1882 that just thirteen days after the South Shields meeting, sixteen representatives from eight clubs arrived effectively to create the Durham County Cricket Club. R.F. Crosthwaite and T.F. Wilson represented South Shields; J.M. Horsley took the chair, while his colleague from Darlington, R.H. Mallett, was to become the second honorary secretary of Durham and then the captain. E.B. Brutton and R.W. Armstrong were there, from Durham School Cricket Club, as were W. Fairbanks and R.T.H. Weatherall, from Durham City. From Stockton came H. Sanderson and T.C. Spence. T. Dobson and A. Grundy were the Whitburn representatives, with H. Geipel and R. Thompson from Gateshead Fell. Along with J.E. White from North Durham came T.E. Main, who was elected as the first officer of the club in the capacities of honorary secretary and honorary treasurer.

Thomas Main's election was item five on that first agenda. Item one deemed that 'a County Club for Durham be formed'. The committee was to comprise a representative of each club, while subscriptions were fixed at a guinea – the currency of sport in those times. No self-respecting club would wait long to appoint some local worthy –

preferably interested in the game but always wealthy – as president. It was item four before they got round to inviting Sir Hedworth Williamson, Bart., of Whitburn Hall, to fill the position. He was said to be 'a good cricketer when a younger man', while his son, Frederick, was to play one match for the county in 1899. That was some thirteen years after his father had ceased to be president, so the young Frederick might well have deserved his place, rather than being given a game just to please his enthusiastic father.

The final item on that first agenda read as follows: 'A deputation from this Club wait upon the Sunderland Committee and explain that a County club has been formed, and make arrangements for the forthcoming County match – Durham v. Northumberland at Sunderland, on the 12 and 13 June, 1882.' Some people in cricket thought that Durham's elevation to first-class status was a whirlwind affair, taking only a couple of years or so from proposal to acceptance. Those fearless and purposeful Victorians had staged a county match within three weeks of forming the club.

A century later, Brian Hunt – appointed as Durham's scorer/statistician for their first season in the County Championship – produced *100 Years of Durham County Cricket Club*. Among the other invaluable information therein is the scorecard for that very first county match (see page 4).

The efficiency of administration seen in organising the match appears to have fallen away somewhat by the first morning. Or perhaps, in those days, not quite so much attention was paid to the need for a prompt start. The remarks at the foot of the scorecard make fascinating reading for the modern-day cricket enthusiast: 'The game was timed to start at 11.30 but as usual there was a considerable

DURHAM CCC v. NORTHUMBERLAND CCC
at Chester Road Ground, Sunderland, 12, 13 June 1882

NORTHUMBERLAND 1st innings / **2nd innings**

Batsman	1st dismissal	bowler	R	2nd dismissal	bowler	R
Bookless, D.	c Pease	b Mewburn	3		b Mewburn	5
S.J. Crawford	lbw	b Thompson	0	lbw	b Mewburn	0
J.F. Ogilvie		b Whyman	26		b Green	48
Foreman, J.		b Whyman	9	c Hutton	b Mewburn	67
T. Raine	c Scott	b Green	25	c H. Thompson	b Mewburn	12
J.A. Hutton		b Crosby	16		b Mewburn	0
E.W. Lilley		b Green	0		b Mewburn	1
J. Scott		b Crosby	11	c Crosby	b Mewburn	10
F. Carr		b Crosby	6	not out		12
C. Liddell	not out		0	absent		0
only 10 men						
Extras			3			7
TOTAL	(for 9 wkts)		99	(for 8 wkts)		162

Bowling	O	M	R	W	O	M	R	W
Thomson, T.	14	5	26	1	11	2	41	0
Mewburn	8	2	17	1	25.3	8	31	7
Crosby	15.1	10	12	3				
Whyman	7	1	20	2	6	1	23	0
Green	16	7	21	2	8	1	32	1

DURHAM 1st innings / **2nd innings**

Batsman	1st dismissal	bowler	R	2nd dismissal	bowler	R
J.A. Pease	c Raine	b Carr	15		b Bookless	0
Thompson, T.		b Crawford	51		b Ogilvie	3
Hutton, H.		b Carr	0		b Crawford	8
A.B. Crosby	c Ogilvie	b Crawford	37	c sub (Scott)	b Bookless	4
Thompson, H.		b Crawford	1	c Foreman	b Crawford	0
J.F. Weatherley	c Raine	b Bookless	40		b Bookless	0
W. Scott	lbw	b Foreman	4	not out		9
T.F. Williams	lbw	b Crawford	25			
J.E. Whyman	c Bookless	b Crawford	0			
C.R. Green		c & b Foreman	0			
A.A.W. Mewburn	not out		3	not out		47
Extras			12			4
TOTAL	(for 10 wkts)		188	(for 6 wkts)		75

Bowling	O	M	R	W	O	M	R	W
Bookless	25.2	4	35	1	20	8	31	3
Crawford	23	6	41	5	6	2	11	2
Raine	13	3	28	0	4	1	4	0
Carr	12	2	21	2	2	0	4	0
Foreman	14	2	31	2				

Umpires: William Cail & Martin McIntyre **DURHAM WON BY 4 WICKETS** delay before the field was set and it was 12.45 before a start was made. J.A. Pease hurt his hand while keeping wicket and W. Scott took his place. J.E. Shilton, the Sunderland pro., acted as second substitute for Northumberland.'

So, Durham's entry into county cricket was delayed by an hour and a quarter – perhaps to allow Northumberland time to find their missing number eleven. If so, it was a fruitless wait, for they took the field with ten men, only to lose Liddell somewhere along the way. It appears that Walter Scott fielded as substitute for the missing man, while the local professional was recruited to cover for Liddell. Despite their lack of numbers, Northumberland made Durham fight all the way for that first victory.

One can only imagine the atmosphere in the Durham camp as wickets fell in the second innings. Only 74 runs needed. A formality, surely? The men of Durham learned in their very first match that there is no such thing as a formality in cricket. They lost wickets cheaply and there was little batting to come. After Williams – playing in his sole county match – there were only Whyman and Green to come, and both were in line to become the first Durham men to bag a 'pair'. Still at the wicket, however, was the captain, Arthur Adolphus William Mewburn.

On the first day of the match the Durham committee had met at the Queen's Hotel in Sunderland. Despite the injured hand that prevented him from keeping wicket, the twenty-two-year-old Joseph Pease had taken the chair. Little business was discussed. They invited some ten worthies to become vice-presidents of the club; they appointed a subcommittee to compile a set of rules by which the club would be governed; and they named A.A.W. Mewburn captain for the season.

It was an inspired choice, for if there had been such a modern irrelevance as a man-of-the-match award in 1882,

Arthur Mewburn would have walked away with it. Tidy bowling in the first innings and a modest score at number eleven were followed by a supreme effort in the second innings. Having destroyed the Northumberland batting in their second innings with 7 for 59, he strode to the wicket to save Durham. An undefeated 47, while none of his colleagues could reach double figures, steered his side to victory and secured a personal triumph for himself.

Known as A.A. Mewburn – he never employed the third initial – Durham's first captain was born in Darlington in 1851. Sunderland was his club, although he could sometimes be found appearing for Durham City or Tyneside Wanderers, and he was an accomplished all-round sportsman. He resigned the captaincy after one season, and the entry for 1883 in the list of captains contains the words 'Chosen of Field'. Mewburn was back for 1884, before finally giving way to Joseph Pease after the 1885 season. He continued playing for Durham until 1892, scoring 731 runs at an average of only 16.24, but he did take 133 off the Yorkshire Gentlemen attack in 1884. He took exactly 100 wickets for the county, while never improving on his figures in that first match against Northumberland. He died at the age of fifty, four years before his son, Bowyer Bell Mewburn, played his solitary match for Durham.

Coincidentally, it was in 1882, the year Durham County Cricket Club was founded, that a cricket record, which still stands today, was established in Durham. Anyone looking through the section headed 'Miscellaneous' in the 'Cricket Records' section of *Wisden* may come across an item that deals with throwing the cricket ball. The entry reads: '140 yards 2 feet, Robert Percival, on the Durham Sands, Co. Durham Racecourse c. 1882.'

The validity of this record has been questioned on more than a few occasions in recent times. The mere fact that the date is listed as 'c. 1882' gives rise to a certain degree of doubt. Percival's achievement exceeds by fifteen inches the previous record, established by Ross Mackenzie in Toronto in 1872. However, local newspapers in 1882 carry no mention of a new world record by a Durham man. There is also some confusion over the venue. Durham Racecourse has always been situated on the site of the present university cricket ground, while the Sands is a grassy area, albeit on sandy soil, further upstream and closer to the city. It has traditionally been the venue for the Durham Easter fairs.

Some light is cast on this cricketing mystery by a letter to *The Sportsman* of 27 March 1889, which mentions Robert Percival being a professional with New Brighton Cricket Club. It goes on to record the famous throw as taking place on Easter Monday 1884, at the Racecourse, in an athletic meeting promoted by the race committee. Apparently, the throw was wind assisted – in modern athletic parlance – and Robert Percival made quite a habit of this sort of thing. He had competed in some twenty similar events in the north-east and had never been beaten at throwing the cricket ball.

Durham men might have been breaking records and Durham County Cricket Club might have been up and running, but it was no easy thing to keep it going in those early days. It proved difficult to develop a regular fixture list and the county lost momentum owing to the haphazard nature of its existence. As is so often the case, it fell to one man to supply the initiative and hard work to see the club through a difficult period. In 1887 Richard Mallett took over as honorary secretary.

Originally from the Potteries, Richard Mallett became a great champion of the Durham cause. He played for Darlington and then Seaham Harbour, and while in his administrative role went to great lengths to build up the fixture list. Furthermore, he always sought out the best fixtures, travelling far and wide to secure first-class opposition whenever possible. He later moved to London, and in 1898 became honorary secretary of the Minor Counties Cricket Association, in which capacity he continued to have Durham's interests very much at heart. Between 1909 and 1931 he was chairman of the association and in 1937 he became its first president, a post he held until his death in November 1939.

Mallett's was a very full cricketing life. Apart from his connections with Durham and work with the Minor Counties, he also managed the MCC side that toured the West Indies in 1929. The Honourable F.S.G. Calthorpe was captain of the England team that halved the four-match series at one game all, with two drawn. Mallett obviously made a favourable impression on the West Indian authorities, for the following year he was asked to manage the West Indies on their first tour of Australia. They lost that series by four matches to one, but there is nothing in the records to suggest that the management was anything other than first class.

It was around the time that Mallett was looking after the administration of Durham that serious moves were afoot regarding the structure of the game in England. In 1887 a County Cricket Council was formed to run the game. After a couple of years, this body suggested a three-tier county championship. Durham were to be assigned third-class status, but the scheme was never implemented, owing to disagreements over promotion and relegation. In December 1890 the idea was suspended indefinitely.

A first-class county championship of sorts had been running since 1864, with the outcome usually decided by the fewest number of matches lost. In 1888 a points system was introduced, albeit unofficially, and in 1890 the championship formally came into being. In 1894 the minor counties, or second-class counties as they were then known, met to discuss the part they had to play in English cricket. Richard Mallett represented Durham at the meeting at Lord's on 11 December from which the Minor Counties Championship developed.

The first championship season was in 1895. To be eligible for consideration, minor counties had to play at least four home and four away matches. A point was awarded for every game won, and a defeat resulted in the deduction of a point. Hence, four of the seven counties that qualified for the final table finished with a negative points tally. That table read:

	P	W	L	D	Pts
Durham	8	4	1	3	3
Norfolk	8	4	1	3	3
Worcestershire	10	5	2	3	3
Bedfordshire	8	3	4	1	-1
Oxfordshire	8	2	3	3	-1
Hertfordshire	8	2	4	2	-2
Staffordshire	8	0	4	4	-4

As ever, *Wisden* had something to say on the matter: 'The struggle for supremacy was very keen, three counties earning the same number of points. The official ruling of the MCC, however, as applied to the first-class counties, would divide the honour of first place between Durham and Norfolk, whose records are identical while their proportion of wins to matches finished is fractionally better than that of Worcestershire.'

It should be said that how the first-class counties separated teams with the same number of points was irrelevant. That was not how the Minor Counties Championship worked and, in modern times, *Wisden*, and everyone else, has indicated that the 1895 Minor Counties

Championship was shared between Durham, Norfolk and Worcestershire.

The following year, Durham could not arrange a sufficient number of fixtures to qualify for the competition. They were back in 1897, out in 1898, but in 1899 they were back for good. Apart from the two World Wars, when competition was suspended, Durham appeared in every Minor Counties Championship until 1992.

It is not within the scope of this book to detail all the achievements of those years, but one is worthy of mention and stands to illustrate how successful the county was. On 30 August 1976, Durham lost by 2 wickets to Northumberland at Jesmond. On 19 August 1982, they lost again by 2 wickets, this time to Staffordshire, at Stockton. In the intervening period Durham went sixty-five Minor Counties Championship matches without defeat, eclipsing the record of Surrey II, who were undefeated in forty-four matches between 1953 and 1956. Durham won thirty of those matches, with twenty-eight drawn and seven reaching no conclusion. In those golden years from 1976 to 1982 their positions in the table were first, second, second, second, first, first and ninth.

It is a proud boast that Durham County Cricket Club left the Minor Counties Championship with a record bettered by no other county. Only Buckinghamshire could match the nine championship-winning years that Durham enjoyed as a minor county. Such successes always reflect a team effort, of course, but in cricket it is the captain who takes much of the credit for a victorious year. Durham might have had nine successful Minor Counties campaigns, but only six men led those sides.

It is often said that bowlers do not make good captains, but the man who led Durham to a share of the first Minor Counties Championship in 1895 was a good bowler and a good captain. William Whitwell bowled right-arm medium pace and achieved a great deal of personal success. He appeared for the county on sixty-nine occasions between 1887 and 1902, captaining the side from 1893 until 1896. He took 355 wickets at an average of only 15.21, many of those victims falling to his off-cutter. He claimed 5 wickets in an innings thirty-two times, and fifteen times took 10 wickets in a match. In 1895 he recorded his best bowling analysis, 8 for 18 against Lincolnshire, and his highest score for Durham, 69 against Staffordshire.

Despite the fact that he was born at Stockton-on-Tees, Whitwell had played ten matches for Yorkshire in 1890, with a certain amount of success. Another great adopted Yorkshireman, Lord Hawke, obviously forgave him for being born outside Yorkshire, for he took him with his touring side to North America in 1894.

William Whitwell's younger brother, Joseph, captained Durham from 1899 until 1902 when, like his brother, he ceased playing county cricket. He had begun his career ten years before taking over the captaincy and he also had played for Yorkshire in 1890. Unlike his brother, however, Joseph was a 'legitimate' Yorkshireman, having been born at Saltburn-by-Sea. He might have captained Durham for only four seasons, with moderate personal success as an opening batsman, but he could claim two Minor Counties Championship years in that short time – 1900 and 1901.

It was not until 1926 that the championship title returned to Durham. The captain then was Bertie Brooks, a legendary batsman and leg-break bowler from Sunderland. His Durham career stretched over 121 matches from 1906 until 1929, in the course of which he scored over 3,000 runs, with two centuries, both in 1922. His championship season came in the middle of his spell in charge, from 1924 to 1928.

Durham were next champions in 1930, when a wicket-keeper batsman, Henry Ferens, was captain. He only appeared sixty-one times for the county, between 1923 and 1931, but he was captain between 1929 and 1931. He was educated at Durham School and captained the Durham City club for twenty-four years before becoming chairman, for thirty-five years, and then president. He went on to become treasurer of Durham County Cricket Club and subsequently chairman. His administrative abilities were not confined to cricket; he was Mayor of Durham and later was awarded the CBE.

After Ferens' brief reign, Durham suffered long years in the wilderness, as far as actually taking the title was concerned. The next championship was not claimed until 1976, when the captain was Brian Lander. He was a true all-rounder. He was a shrewd leader, a batsman, a medium-pace bowler, possessed as safe a pair of hands as could be wished for, and for five years appeared in the Minor Counties representative side. Having made his debut in 1963, he played for the county until 1986, and was captain between 1973 and 1979. It was a reign blessed with success and near misses, for apart from winning the championship itself in 1976, Durham were runners-up in 1977, 1978 and 1979.

This was the start of Durham's most successful period in the Minor Counties Championship. The title was secured again in 1980, 1981 and 1984, and on each occasion the captain was Neil Riddell. A stocky, left-handed batsman, he made his Durham debut in 1972, took over the captaincy in 1980 and did not stand down until the end of the 1990 season, when he had made a record 218 appearances. In that time he scored very nearly 8,000 runs in the Minor Counties Championship, at an average of 37.69, and in 1978 finished top of the Minor Counties batting averages.

He was a member of the Minor Counties representative side between 1976 and 1987, and for three years, from 1985 to 1987, was its captain. He marked his debut for Minor Counties (East) in the Benson & Hedges Cup competition in 1976 by scoring an undefeated 109 in just over two hours, including eight 6s and nine 4s, against a Northamptonshire attack that included Test bowlers Sarfraz Nawaz, Bob Cottam, Bishen Bedi and Peter Willey.

The nature of the Minor Counties Championship has changed considerably over the years. In recent times it has been divided into Eastern and Western divisions, with a limited-overs play-off match between the winners of the two divisions to decide the title of Minor Counties Champions. Another development was the introduction in 1983 of a one-day limited-overs competition for the minor counties. Durham achieved just one success in this knock-out cup. That came in 1984, when Neil Riddell's side beat Dorset in the final.

Prior to their gaining first-class status, Durham's achievements were not confined to the minor-counties competitions. Between 1901 and 1962 the county were granted fixtures against the major overseas touring teams. Quite why Durham, alone among individual minor counties, should have received this honour is not clear. Perhaps Richard Mallett had something to do with it. Remembering the difficulties he overcame in arranging suitable fixtures while he was honorary secretary of Durham, it is possible that he used his influence at Lord's to secure the first match against the touring South Africans in 1901. Whatever, once Durham were on the tourists' fixture list, like so much in cricket, this was never changed, because it was never questioned.

That first match in 1901 was played over three days in June at the Feethams Ground in Darlington, and was a rather one-sided affair. Durham did well enough to bowl out the South Africans for 225 in their first innings. The county's reply started well enough, reaching 116 for 3 at one stage, before falling to 188 all out. It was then that the tourists made their class and strength tell. In their second innings they amassed 502 for 9 declared. A demoralised Durham slumped to 29 for 8, before a token recovery saw them to 93 all out. The South Africans' margin of victory was 446 runs.

Another South African team appeared at Ashbrooke, Sunderland, in 1907, and the result was much the same. The tourists won by an innings and 29 runs. To entertain the crowd, the South Africans batted a second time in an exhibition innings. They reached 139 for 8, with seven wickets falling to the slow left-arm bowling of Charles Adamson. Very much a local man, Adamson was born in Durham, went to Durham School and played for Durham City. He had gone to Australia in 1898 with the British Lions and stayed on after the rugby tour to play cricket. He appeared once for Queensland in first-class cricket before returning to captain Durham between 1912 and the outbreak of the First World War. He was killed in action a few months before the cessation of hostilities in 1918.

The Ashbrooke ground became the established venue for tourist matches. Durham took a first-innings lead against All India in 1911, before losing by 8 wickets. The following year they had a deficit of 207 on the first innings when rain ruined the first match against the Australians. This was the first of four matches that Johnny Common played against senior touring teams. He was a highly proficient wicket-keeper and, in county cricket, a capable batsman. His batting ability was not evident on the 'international' stage, however, for he recorded scores of 0, 0, 5, 8 not out, 0, and 0 in those four outings. As a wicket-keeper his tally was just one catch and one stumping. His brother, Alf Common, made an indelible mark in the world of Association Football by becoming the first man to command a £1,000 transfer fee, when he moved from Sunderland to Middlesbrough in 1905.

The Australians returned in 1921 to record a 10-wicket victory, while the West Indians were first received at Feethams in 1923. The team from the Caribbean won by 180 runs, bowling out Durham for just 63 and 74. In 1924 Durham gained a first-innings lead of 22 against the South Africans at Sunderland, and were 12 for no wicket in their second innings when rain caused the abandonment of the match. Two years later, the Australians lost only 3 wickets in winning by an innings and 81 runs.

There was a first meeting with New Zealand in 1927, at Ropery Lane, Chester-le-Street. Although the tourists won by 10 wickets, Durham produced an outstanding individual performance from John Cook. Essentially a bowler, he came in at number ten, when Durham were 58 for 8 in reply to New Zealand's 373, and proceeded to score a century in a partnership of 195 with Bertie Brooks. It was a new ninth-wicket record for the county, and Cook, who had taken 4 wickets in the New Zealand first innings, became the first Durham man to take a century off a touring side.

At Sunderland, in 1928, Durham played out a most honourable draw with the West Indies. At the close the West Indies were 61 for 3 in their second innings, chasing 143 to win. This time the Durham hero was Thomas Dobson Jr, one of the best all-rounders ever to appear for the county, and from one of its finest cricketing families. Thomas Dobson Sr played for Durham, as did three of his brothers and Thomas Jr's brother William. On 1 June 1928, Thomas Dobson Jr went to the wicket with Durham in a precarious position at 28 for 4. He played a magnificent innings of 105, the first of his five centuries for the county.

A heavy defeat by the South Africans in 1929 was followed by a rain-affected draw against New Zealand in 1931. In 1933, however, the West Indies undoubtedly had the worse of a draw at Sunderland. Charlie Adamson, the son of Charles Adamson, who had taken those South African wickets in 1907, and grandson of another Durham player and administrator, John Adamson, was top-scorer with 93, as Durham reached 256. The West Indies made only 140 in reply and, following on, were 29 for 3 at the close.

Durham did well to hang on for a draw against the 1934 Australians, but suffered a heavy defeat at the hands of the 1935 South Africans. A fairly depressing pattern had developed in these matches between Durham and touring sides, with the county generally being outplayed, with only the occasional relief of a draw. That pattern, however, was dramatically broken in 1936.

India went to Ashbrooke under the captaincy of the man who became Sir Gajapatairaj Vijaya Ananda – the Maharajkumar of Vizianagram while in England. Fortunately for all concerned, and especially the scorers, he was known simply as Maharaja Vizianagram when in Sunderland. His side was a good one, containing the likes of Vijay Merchant and Lala Amarnath. Exactly forty years later, Lala Amarnath's son Mohinder was engaged as professional by South Shields and played for Durham with distinction for three seasons. In his twenty-eight innings for the county, Jimmy, as he was always known, scored five centuries and three 50s, as well as taking wickets. He was also a very popular member of the side and it was widely acclaimed in the north-east when he took the man-of-the-match award in the 1983 World Cup final as India beat the West Indies at Lord's.

India batted first in the 1936 match, scoring 174, and Durham managed a lead of just two runs on the first innings, thanks largely to an undefeated half-century from the captain, Thomas Dobson, going in at number eight. Wazir Ali hit 139 not out in India's second innings, as the Maharaja declared with 3 wickets down and Durham needing 202 to win. Parnaby and Randle put on 109 for the first wicket and Durham recorded a famous victory, with 5 wickets in hand.

That was the year one of the most distinguished characters ever to play for Durham made his debut. Arthur Austin was reckoned to be without peer as a wicket-keeper between 1936 and 1954. When it comes to catches, wicket-keepers are judged on those they miss rather than those they take. Arthur Austin missed very few, and as for stumpings, he was in a class of his own. Of the 129 dismissals he claimed in his sixty matches for Durham, 67 were caught and 62 stumped. Records do not disclose how many of those stumpings were down the leg side, where he was quite breathtaking in his brilliance. He joined the committee in 1950, while still an active cricketer, and took up the post of secretary in 1969. He became chairman in 1975 and still held that position when Durham were granted first-class status. And Arthur Austin was by no means merely a figurehead as chairman. He has rarely missed a Durham match at home or away and occupies a very special place in the affections of Durham cricket followers.

In 1937 it was the turn of the New Zealanders to visit Ashbrooke. Walter Hadlee was in the visiting side, as was Martin Donnelly, but Durham too had a Test cricketer to put into the field. Their captain was David Townsend, the last man from a minor-county team to appear for England in a Test Match. He never did represent a first-class county. He had appeared for Oxford University in 1933 and 1934, scoring 193 in his last Varsity Match. The following winter he went to the West Indies with R.E.S. Wyatt's side. He played in three Tests, and while he did not sparkle as an opening batsman in his six innings, he certainly flourished when he returned to make his Durham debut in 1935.

The 1937 season saw the start of a term of captaincy that lasted until 1947, and David Townsend marked it with the highest score of his career against that New Zealand attack. His undefeated 138 stood between Durham and another disaster. He did not bat in the second innings as the county, chasing 220 to win, reached 100 for 4 by the close.

Durham were to play a further nine matches against touring sides as a minor county. Never again were they to cause an upset. Even so, there were some notable individual performances by Durham players in these matches. Keith Jackson opened the bowling against the all-conquering 1948 Australians and took 5 for 76 in 29 overs in front of 18,000 spectators. He also top-scored with 23 and claimed a 4-wicket haul against the 1950 West Indians.

That 1950 match was notable for the performance of Jackie Keeler. Opening the batting, he scored 90 in the first innings before falling to the occasional off-breaks of Roy Marshall. In the second innings, Keeler had reached 97 when Marshall struck again. Two years later, when India were the visitors, Jackie Keeler scored 135, as Durham came close to embarrassing the tourists. Two Yorkshire exiles, Alex Coxon and Ron Aspinall, took 4 and 6 wickets, respectively, as India were forced to follow on. They were still 45 runs behind with 3 wickets down in the second innings at close of play.

When India returned to Sunderland in 1959, Durham again had the better of a drawn match. The county's first innings of 267 for 8 declared was built around the sturdy frame of Colin Milburn, who hit a magnificent century on his debut. The man who was to be such a great entertainer for England, Northamptonshire and Western Australia played only three more innings for Durham. He scored 12 in the second knock against the Indians, followed by 10 and 11 when he appeared once in the Durham side of 1976 that won the Minor Counties Championship. By then, of course, he had lost an eye in a motor accident and was no longer the batsman who could totally dominate any attack in the world on his day.

Colin Milburn was capable of putting almost every other player in the shade – physically and metaphorically. Jack Watson must have felt that as, after Milburn's attention-grabbing performance, he returned the remarkable figures of 15.2-7-23-6 in the Indian first innings. Set 239 to win, in what turned out to be 48 overs, India were 210 for 7 at the end, with Watson taking three more wickets.

The final match Durham played against a touring side as a minor county was in 1962, when their opponents were Pakistan. Again, it was a rain-ruined event, though it did produce a century for Durham's David Ellis.

It was somehow fitting that in the year Durham made their debut in the ranks of the first-class counties, the touring country should again be Pakistan. The series of matches interrupted in 1962 was scheduled to be resumed against the same opposition at Chester-le-Street, exactly thirty years later.

In the meantime, Durham had featured strongly in another famous tourist match. In 1977 the Australians travelled to Sunderland to meet a Minor Counties representative XI. After a somewhat generous declaration by Australia's Doug Walters, the Minor Counties won by 6 wickets. Durham's Neil Riddell was at the crease when the winning run was scored, after his county colleague Stuart Wilkinson had taken 4 wickets in the Australians' first innings. Peter Kippax also played in that match, but at the time represented Northumberland. By the following season, the leg-spinning all-rounder was a Durham player and appeared for the Minor Counties XI again when they beat New Zealand at Torquay. Also in that side were Stuart Wilkinson and Steve Atkinson, another prolific batsman for Durham.

If playing against touring teams helped to keep Durham County Cricket Club in the public eye, performances in the Gillette Cup/NatWest Trophy competition shot the county to far greater prominence.

Cricket followers are no different from the rest of the population of the British Isles in that they love a sporting underdog – that is, unless the underdog happens to be playing their team, when the affection turns to foreboding. In the 60-overs-a-side knock-out competition, Durham have shown why that foreboding exists.

Durham first appeared in the competition in 1964, as one of the five leading minor counties from the 1963 season. Their participation was an innovation in the second year of the Gillette Cup, giving the potential for the sort of David-and-Goliath upset that enlivens the FA Cup but which did not actually occur in the Gillette until 1973. The fates decreed that Durham should meet one of the other minor counties, Hertfordshire, in the first round in 1964. Durham won by 7 wickets and Stuart Young, reputed to be 'the best fast bowler in the country never to play county cricket', won the man-of-the-match award with figures of 8.4-5-13-4. Young took another three wickets in the second round as Durham lost to Sussex by 200 runs.

In succeeding seasons, Durham came close to causing the type of upset the sponsors no doubt had in mind when

GILLETTE CUP
(1st round)
YORKSHIRE v. DURHAM
at St George's Road, Harrogate, 30 June 1973

YORKSHIRE

*G. Boycott		b Wilkinson	14
R.G. Lumb	c Old	b Lander	4
P.J. Sharpe	c Cole	b Inglis	12
J.H. Hampshire	c Inglis	b Lander	10
C. Johnson	hit wicket	b Greensword	44
R.A. Hutton		b Lander	0
C.M. Old		b March	5
D.L. Bairstow	lbw	b Greensword	11
P. Carrick		b Lander	18
H.P. Cooper	not out		10
A.G. Nicholson		b Lander	0
	Extras (1 b, 6 lb)		7

TOTAL (for 10 wkts)   135 (58.4 overs)

Fall of wickets: 1–18, 2–32, 3–34, 4–49, 5–49, 6–80, 7–100, 8–121, 9–135, 10–135

Bowling	O	M	R	W
Wilkinson	12	3	33	1
Old	7	2	10	0
Lander	11.4	3	15	5
Inglis	8	3	23	1
March	8	3	18	1
Greensword	12	4	29	2

DURHAM

R. Inglis	c Cooper	b Carrick	47
S.R. Atkinson	c &	b Carrick	14
S. Greensword	not out		35
J.G. March	run out		7
A.G.B. Old	c Bairstow	b Cooper	6
N.A. Riddell		b Nicholson	15
D.W. Soakell	not out		10
P.J. Crane			
*B.R. Lander			
J.S. Wilkinson			
R. Cole			
	Extras (4 lb)		4

TOTAL (for 5 wkts)   138 (51.3 overs)

Fall of wickets: 1–58, 2–63, 3–87, 4–96, 5–123

Bowling	O	M	R	W
Old	8	1	15	0
Nicholson	11.3	3	27	1
Cooper	12	3	25	1
Carrick	12	4	32	2
Hutton	8	1	35	0

Umpires: C.S. Elliott & A. Jepson
Man of the match: B.R. Lander   **DURHAM WON BY 5 WICKETS**

the invitation to the minor counties was first extended. The captain, John Bailey, took the individual award as Durham lost to Nottinghamshire by just 11 runs in 1967. Bailey scored 30 and took 3 for 37 in 12 overs, all of them clean bowled. Stuart Young collected another medal for the admirable return of 12-3-17-4, as Worcestershire won a low-scoring match in 1968 by 16 runs.

Durham did not qualify for the competition again until 1972, when they returned with a first-round victory over Oxfordshire. Alan Burridge, later to become secretary of Middlesex, took the man-of-the-match award for a splendid 95, after the much-travelled Dave Halfyard had taken 2 for 11 off 12 overs. Surrey overwhelmed Durham in the second round.

In 1973, Durham were drawn to play Yorkshire at Harrogate in the first round. Yorkshire, whose side included six Test players, had reached the final of the Benson & Hedges Cup the previous year, and must have been looking ahead to a second-round match against Essex. Yet, in that second round, Essex had to travel to Chester-le-Street, for Durham had shocked the cricketing world by beating Yorkshire by 5 wickets.

Durham's captain at that time was Brian Lander, a most competent all-round cricketer and a fine leader. On that famous day in June 1973, he played a crucial part in the county's victory, not only by his captaincy but with one of the outstanding spells of bowling in the history of the competition.

Yorkshire won the toss, batted, and faced a tight opening attack of Stuart Wilkinson and Alan Old, an England rugby union international, who was playing against his more famous cricketing brother, Chris, in the Yorkshire side. Only 18 runs came from the first 9 overs of the innings and then the mighty Boycott's wicket fell. The fielding side was inspired, and none more so than the captain. Brian Lander brought himself into the attack. Wickets fell at regular intervals and Durham were left with plenty of time to chase a modest total. Russell Inglis and Steve Atkinson did more than just withstand the opening assault, and Steve Greensword piloted Durham to the target with 8.5 overs and 5 wickets to spare.

The scorecard (page 21) merely records the facts and figures. It cannot convey the spirit of the Durham side, the magnitude of the achievement, or the sense of history that was abroad that day. Like any sporting first, it showed others what could be achieved.

Before Roger Bannister broke the four-minute mile barrier, there were those who doubted it could be done. It needed someone with the foresight, belief and inner determination to go out and actually run a mile, not in 4 minutes, but in 3 minutes 59.99 seconds or less. It is the first breaching of that barrier – which is as much psychological as physical – that is so important.

Other minor counties had come close to beating first-class opposition. However, the fact that such a result had never quite been achieved left self-doubt, which grew into the expectation of defeat in the minds of the players. Durham overcame those doubts and fears. Once they had done so, the sneaking suspicion that there was some concealed special clause in the Laws of Cricket, stating that a minor county will never defeat a first-class county in a limited-overs match, was banished for ever.

Durham themselves moved on to maintain the fine record they had established in the Gillette Cup and to carry the flag of Minor Counties cricket into first-class realms. They met with no further success in their 1973 campaign, falling to Essex in the next round. They won their first-round match in 1974, getting the better of Hertfordshire by 74 runs. John

Stoker's 3 for 16 off 12 overs earned another individual award for a Durham player. Again the run ended in the second round, this time at the hands of Kent.

Stuart Wilkinson won another man-of-the-match award in 1977, when Durham lost to Northamptonshire by just 3 wickets. Bearing in mind that only Bishen Bedi and John Dye were still to bat, Northamptonshire had little margin for error. The irony was that the end of their innings was held together by George Sharp, a native of West Hartlepool.

The 1978 draw saw a repeat of the historic 1973 tie between Durham and Yorkshire. There was no repeat of the result, however. Strangely enough, the two met again in 1979. It was a second-round tie, which Yorkshire won, after Durham had beaten Berkshire. Yet another man-of-the-match award was won by a Durham man in that first-round match. Steve Greensword received the honour after scoring 48 not out and taking 1 for 20 in his 12 overs. Making his debut in the competition for Durham in the game against Berkshire was Paul Romaines. He had played for Northamptonshire for a couple of seasons before returning to his native north-east to appear with Durham. He then went off to play for Gloucestershire, going back home for a short time to take up a post as commercial manager with Durham when they were granted first-class status.

At the beginning of the 1980s Durham could call upon the services of two high-quality overseas Test players, Wasim Raja of Pakistan and Lance Cairns of New Zealand. Both had been playing in the leagues and now committed themselves to the Durham cause. Wasim Raja was adjudged the man of the match when Durham went to Trent Bridge to meet Nottinghamshire in 1980. This was the last year of Gillette's sponsorship of the 60-overs

NATWEST TROPHY
(1st Round)

DERBYSHIRE v. DURHAM
at Derby, 3 July 1985

DERBYSHIRE

*K.J. Barnett		b Patel	53
I.S. Anderson	c Fothergill	b Johnson	4
J.E. Morris		b Johnson	12
B. Roberts	c Fothergill	b Patel	13
R. Sharma	c Johnson	b Patel	11
G. Miller	c Hurst	b Greensword	0
M.A. Holding	lbw	b Greensword	27
P.G. Newman	c Riddell	b Johnston	19
+B.J.M. Maher	c Johnson	b Greensword	0
A.E. Warner		b Johnston	17
O.H. Mortensen	not out		4
	Extras (5 lb, 6 w)		11

TOTAL (for 10 wkts)   171 (58.4 overs)

Fall of wickets: 1–14, 2–40, 3–83, 4–94, 5–99, 6–99, 7–142, 8–144, 9–158, 10–171

Bowling	O	M	R	W
Scott	8	1	29	0
Johnston	11.4	2	31	2
Johnson	12	0	35	2
Burn	3	0	17	0
Patel	12	3	34	3
Greensword	12	4	20	3

DURHAM

J.W. Lister	c Roberts	b Holding	42
D.C. Jackson	lbw	b Warner	0
S. Greensword	c Roberts	b Holding	40
*N.A. Riddell	not out		49
A.S. Patel	not out		21
G. Hurst			
P. Burn			
+A.R. Fothergill			
G. Johnson			
A.W. Scott			
J. Johnston			
	Extras (1 b, 12 lb, 5 w, 2 nb)		20

TOTAL (for 3 wkts)   172 (55.4 overs)

Fall of wickets: 1–62, 2–63, 3–114

Bowling	O	M	R	W
Holding	12	2	36	1
Warner	12	1	46	1
Newman	12	0	25	0
Mortensen	10.4	2	37	1
Miller	9	4	15	0

Umpires: J.H. Harris & D.O. Oslear
Man of the match: S. Greensword   **DURHAM WON BY 7 WICKETS**

competition, which became the NatWest Trophy in 1981. That year, Durham lost to Lancashire at Old Trafford, and in 1982 were beaten by Surrey at The Oval.

Simon Davis, from the Australian state side Victoria, was in the Durham team that played Lancashire again in 1983. Lancashire won easily, but Davis took the individual award with his 7 for 32, the third-best figures ever recorded in the competition. Steve Greensword added to his and Durham's gold medal collection with a good all-round display against Northamptonshire in 1984.

Since Durham's defeat of Yorkshire in 1973, other minor counties had embarrassed senior sides. Even so, it was still a newsworthy event when Durham beat Derbyshire at Derby in 1985. Having been the first side from the Minor Counties Championship to beat a first-class county in the Gillette Cup, they became the first to claim a similar scalp in the NatWest Trophy. Kent proved too strong for them in the second round, but Durham were now the first minor county to have beaten first-class opposition twice in the premier limited-overs competition.

If they did not manage to record a third such victory, more awards went to individual players. Peter Kippax won one at Darlington against Middlesex in 1987. John Glendenen could have had another in Durham's last season before elevation. He scored 109 against Glamorgan, but Hugh Morris and Matthew Maynard had earlier shared an unbroken partnership of 259 in a record third-wicket partnership. Durham, however, were still in the record business themselves. In that match they became the first minor county to score more than 300 in an innings.

By that time, Durham had, of course, been granted first-class status for 1992. Their path was undoubtedly smoothed by their famous exploits in limited-overs cricket, but they were not enough on their own; many other components had to be in place before the Test and County Cricket Board came to their momentous decision. But the fact that Durham had established a reputation in cup cricket, with those wins over Yorkshire and Derbyshire, and by claiming numerous individual awards and records, meant that opinion had been edged that vital bit closer to accepting them as a first-class county.

2

Cricket in the North-East

Durham County Cricket Club's outstanding record as a minor county is only one aspect of the sporting tradition associated with the north-east of England. Such is the community spirit found in the region as a whole that a sense of close public identification with local sporting personalities and teams reaches unparalleled intensity.

Travel to almost any part of the English-speaking world and you will find somebody who wants to know whether Newcastle United or Sunderland won last Saturday. Whereas natural support for a home-town football club will usually be diluted by long residence in another area, Geordies and Mackems maintain a fervour for their teams that appears to grow in inverse proportion to the distance they are from St James's Park or Roker Park. Furthermore, support for the team is nothing compared with the idolisation reserved for individual sporting heroes.

When Jackie Milburn, one of the greatest of those footballing idols from the north-east, died, his funeral procession brought the people out to line the streets in numbers that might more usually be reserved for royalty. But the likes of Jackie Milburn and Len Shackleton have always been treated like royalty in the north-east. So, too, have those who have followed in recent years, like Kevin Keegan, Chris Waddle and Paul Gascoigne. If the team is doing badly, crowds will be down to a level that is still the envy of more successful teams that do not enjoy the same history and traditions. When a new 'star' appears, or there is the merest hint that the good times are about to return, attendances rocket.

That has been seen in ice-hockey, where the Durham Wasps have become one of the most successful sides in the country, and the public flock to their matches. The success of Brendan Foster as an athlete attracted so much support that, when he developed Gateshead as a major athletics centre, the backing was transferred from him as an individual to his concept of promoting the sport in and for the area. His marketing skills also played no small part in promoting Durham County Cricket Club's first-class ambitions. Meanwhile, his athletic mantle was taken up by the charismatic and even more successful Steve Cram.

This regional phenomenon occurs across the sporting spectrum. A Sunderland boxer, a bantamweight called Billy Hardy, pulled in not only boxing fans when he fought at the Crowtree Leisure Centre in Sunderland; he received support from the north-east sporting public as a whole. There is no obvious affinity between boxing and ice-skating, yet British Ladies Champion Joanne Conway would go to his contests. Quite simply, she was from the north-east, he was from the north-east, so it was natural for her to support him in his endeavours against the rest of the world.

Psychologists and sociologists could no doubt offer learned academic treatises to explain this. They would say it was something to do with tribal identity, a desire to band together to guard against repression by outside forces, I should not wonder. However, to experience the feeling for sport in the north-east is to explain the emotions. There is a good, old-fashioned sentiment in the north-east that means they love their sport; and, loving their sport, they will follow, to a man, woman and child, the sportsmen and women who perform at the top level on their behalf.

Cricket has not been omitted from this sporting culture. If it is only now that there is a first-class county side in which to take an interest, it does not mean there has not always been strong support for good cricket in the north-east. But it is the general sporting sympathy that helped make the dream of a first-class county club in the region a reality.

That there was support for such a move became evident with the introduction of the Callers-Pegasus Cricket Festival. Roy and Ian Caller were typical sports-loving businessmen from Newcastle. The fact that they were successful, initially in the family furniture business and then in travel, meant they could do something to indulge their passion.

In 1977 the Caller firm was celebrating its eightieth anniversary. Sport had to feature in the festivities and it was decided to sponsor a golf tournament on the European tour. Whitley Bay, a downland course of undulating terrain, was the venue for the Callers of Newcastle Open. It was staged over the last four days of July, so the scramble for Ryder Cup qualification points was at its peak, adding a little extra spice to the tournament.

This extra incentive, above and beyond the £25,000 purse, ensured a high-class field. Nick Faldo, Mark James, Sam Torrance and Bernard Gallacher were among the strong British contingent; and the presence of Severiano Ballesteros and Manuel Pinero from Spain, Greg Norman and David Graham from Australia, John Bland and Hugh Baiocchi of South Africa, plus a clutch of Americans and other nationalities, made for a festive occasion. But none of these top players featured in the exciting finale.

Peter Butler and South Africa's John Fourie finished the

fourth round 6 under par. Tommy Horton came to the 17th at 8 under, only to fall away to finish 6 under. His playing partner, Angel Gallardo, was 4 under on the 17th tee, but the Spaniard rose to the occasion to complete a four-way play-off. The two British players went out at the first extra hole, and Fourie defeated Gallardo at the second. It was thrilling golf, and, because there was a major event taking place in the north-east, it was well-supported golf.

The Caller brothers had realised the potential for staging such events in their home area. They had briefly discussed the possibility of a multi-sponsored event to push up the prize money and attract an even better field. It was a policy followed enthusiastically on the American tour, where organisations within a municipality joined together to promote a tournament carrying the district or city's name. Unfortunately, Tyneside did not come up with sufficient backing and the idea fell by the wayside.

The potential for other sponsorships had not, however, escaped the notice of Roy and Ian Caller. Following the celebration of Newcastle's 900th anniversary in 1980, the City Council approached them about the possibility of sponsoring a sporting event. They had been born a matter of yards away from the Northumberland County Cricket Club ground at Jesmond, where the West Indians were playing the Minor Counties representative side in a two-day game at the end of July 1980. Cricket was another great interest of the Callers and they willingly supported the occasion.

For the first time in some twenty-five years the Jesmond ground was full. It was an early indication that the region was ready for the big names of cricket to come north-east. Seven of the West Indian side that had just drawn the fourth Test, and eight of those who were to draw the fifth, took part in the match. In the Minor Counties XI were two Durham players – Steve Greensword and Peter Kippax.

The Durham representatives played their parts to the full. The West Indians were in a strong position at 266 for 2 when, with consecutive deliveries, the leg-spin of Kippax accounted for Timur Mohamed (119) and Alvin Kallicharran (109). He was denied his hat-trick by a certain I.V.A. Richards, but he did claim the great Antiguan's wicket later in the innings. Greensword accounted for Collis King, and proceeded to record the second highest score in the Minor Counties innings, hitting 32. Kippax, with the help of a catch by his Durham team-mate, dismissed King in the second innings before rain washed away the prospect of an interesting finish.

For the first time since the days when Durham played the overseas touring sides, international cricket was back in the north-east. Public support for the game at this level was confirmed. That support deserved to be maintained, and the foundations of the Callers-Pegasus Festival were laid. Every year until 1990, top cricketers from all over the world would be booked to appear in the most northerly cricket festival of its kind in the world.

At the outset, Roy and Ian Caller were not sure how to go about collecting such cricketing talent together for the matches. They wanted the top players, but they had been warned about dealing with managers and agents. Furthermore, they had been badly let down by an unnamed golfer who had gone as far as inspecting his suite at the players' hotel and yet still failed to turn up for the Callers of Newcastle Open. They wanted no repetition of that incident, feeling that if you promise the public the very best, the very best must have a very good excuse not to be there.

As it turned out, not once were they let down, and the annual event became a success in every respect. The players performed at exactly the right level of competitive cricket and behaved impeccably, so that the Callers-Pegasus Festival was a successful social as well as cricketing event. The standards set went a long way towards convincing potential cricket enthusiasts in the north-east that here was another sport worthy of their attention and support.

From the beginning, it was decided that the festival should take a simple but attractive form. An International XI would play a Northumberland & Durham XI. Callers-Pegasus would pay the bills, while the two counties shared the proceeds. Then there was the question of how the players to form the International XI should be recruited. Ken Barrington was chosen as manager and, after a meeting shortly before Christmas 1980, he was ready to undertake the job. The Callers hit it off immediately with Barrington, and were devastated when they heard of his tragic death on tour in the West Indies the following March.

Alec Bedser offered to help in any way he could, and the Callers' introduction to Frank Twiselton, a former chairman and subsequently president of Gloucestershire, proved most valuable. Frank Twiselton had been with the Whitbread Brewery before taking early retirement, and Whitbread sponsored an Old England XI. He used that connection to produce the combined Northumberland & Durham XI's opposition, and the side he came up with almost guaranteed another full house at Jesmond on Thursday 6 August 1981.

Rain delayed the start of what should have been a 55-overs-per-side match until one o'clock, so the overs were reduced to 45. There were no fewer than seven Test captains in the International XI. Two of them, Glenn Turner of New Zealand and England's Geoff Boycott, opened the batting, with a wealth of talent to follow. Desmond Haynes, Basil D'Oliveira, and Ian Botham, fresh from his Headingley triumph against Australia, occupied the next three places in the order. Then came the captain, a Geordie by birth, Tom Graveney, followed by Zaheer Abbas, wicket-keeper David Bairstow, Kapil Dev, Chris Old and Dilip Doshi.

It was not a bad array of batting talent when you think that Kapil Dev, who was to score nearly 5,000 Test runs and seven Test centuries, was due to come in at number nine. Even so, festival or not, Geoff Boycott played it by the book. His 22 took exactly an hour, during which time he faced 44 deliveries. Meanwhile, his opening partner, Glenn Turner, had faced 57 balls in scoring 73, so perhaps there was no reason for Boycott to go mad.

Turner went on to 96, including five 6s and twelve 4s. Basil D'Oliveira chipped in with an undefeated 66, Ian Botham's 42 came from only 33 deliveries, and Zaheer was not out 30 at the closure of the innings. It was not a bad attack they were facing, including Norman Graham, formerly of Kent, Lance Cairns of New Zealand and Wasim Raja of Pakistan.

The Northumberland & Durham XI's reply was opened by Paul Romaines with Steve Atkinson, his regular opening partner for Durham at the time. They had taken 27 off 5 overs delivered by Kapil Dev and Chris Old when the rain returned and the match was abandoned. It was a disappointment for all concerned, but the Callers-Pegasus Festival had been launched. Another match was played the following day, with 84 from man-of-the-match Paul Romaines leading the locals to a 23-run victory over illustrious opposition that now included Mike Gatting in place of D'Oliveira.

The festival retained the same format for another three years. The best cricketers in the world came to represent the International XI, and, for all the efforts of the Minor Counties players, the opposition was just too strong. It was entertaining festival cricket, but rather too one-sided for the discerning north-eastern public to enjoy it to the full – good fun, but not good competition. When the International XI won by only 44 runs in the second match of 1983, it was reckoned to be a close-run thing.

The first match in 1984 was rained off. There was little likelihood of play at any stage, yet the spectators remained in their places, just in case. Tom Graveney remarked that he had never seen so many people waiting patiently in the rain for a cricket match that was not going to start. There was no play until after two o'clock the next afternoon, when the International XI won a 25-over match by 25 runs. The weather in 1984, and the one-sided nature of the contests, resulted in a revamped festival for 1985.

The Callers-Pegasus International XI became the Rest of the World XI, and their opposition was now an England XI. This format remained unchanged and successful until 1990, when the last match was played. By then, Durham County Cricket Club's first-class bid was under way, and all possible energies and resources were channelled into it. The game played by first-class cricketers had found a ready place in the north-east.

At that last fixture in 1990, eleven players briefly took the field each day in addition to those actually playing. The sponsors had celebrated the occasion by inviting, as their guests, an Old England XI. May, Compton, Graveney, Evans, Bailey, Statham, Trueman, Dexter, Cowdrey, Simpson and Lock were introduced to the crowd and received a rousing reception. The local public were aware of the history of the game as well as playing a significant part in its future.

Despite the lack of Callers-Pegasus involvement, the festival continued in 1991 under the banner of Yuill Heritage Homes and as a purely Northumberland-orientated event. The part it had played in the promotion of Durham

FESTIVAL RESULTS

Won by England XI	6
Rest of the World XI	5
International XI	5
Northumberland & Durham XI	1

Two matches were rained off without a ball being bowled and one failed to reach a conclusion.

HIGHEST SCORES

406 all out in 54 overs	by International XI	1982
357 – 9 in 55 overs	by International XI	1982
308 – 3 in 55 overs	by International XI	1983
300 – 6 in 55 overs	by Rest of the World XI	1986
288 all out in 52.3 overs	by Northumberland & Durham XI	1982

LOWEST (all out) SCORE

179 in 50.2 overs by England XI   1990

BEST PARTNERSHIPS

1st	185*	S.J. Cook & M.D. Crowe	Rest of the World XI	1990
2nd	235	G.A. Gooch & A.J. Lamb	International XI	1982
3rd	104	C.G. Greenidge & D.M. Jones	Rest of the World XI	1987
4th	157*	R.G. Pollock & Javed Miandad	International XI	1983
5th	110	A.R. Border & C.G. Greenidge	Rest of the World XI	1986
6th	117	P.J.L. Dujon & R.J. Shastri	Rest of the World XI	1989
7th	95	I.T. Botham & R.M. Ellison	England XI	1986
8th	42*	M.J. Greatbatch & C. Sharma	Rest of the World XI	1989
9th	33	B.N. French & A.P. Igglesden	England XI	1990
10th	25	S.P. Davis & J.N. Graham	N'land & Durham	1982

INDIVIDUAL HUNDREDS

134	A.J. Lamb	International XI	1982
130	G.A. Gooch	International XI	1982
127*	M.W. Gatting	England XI	1985
118*	R.G. Pollock	International XI	1983
115*	M.J. Greatbatch	Rest of the World XI	1989
114	S.R. Atkinson	Northumberland & Durham XI	1983
114	C.G. Greenidge	Rest of the World XI	1986
112*	M.D. Crowe	Rest of the World XI	1990
106	A.J. Lamb	England XI	1986

FASTEST 50 (balls): 25 by G.A. Gooch   International XI   1982
FASTEST 100 (balls): 68 by A.J. Lamb   England XI   1986

BEST BOWLING

5–36	J.N. Graham	Northumberland & Durham XI	1982
4–10	Javed Miandad	Rest of the World XI	1988
4–34	P.R. Sleep	Rest of the World XI	1990
4–35	P.J.W. Allott	England XI	1985
4–38	R.A. Harper	Rest of the World XI	1986
4–38	T.A. Munton	England XI	1990
4–38	C. Sharma	Rest of the World XI	1989
4–40	C.A. Walsh	Rest of the World XI	1989
4–57	J.K. Lever	England XI	1986
4–65	S.P. Davis	Northumberland & Durham XI	1982
4–72	B.L. D'Oliveira	International XI	1982

to first-class status is perhaps summed up best by Graham Gooch. The Essex and England captain wrote an appreciation to Roy and Ian Caller, which appeared in a presentation booklet recording the facts and figures of the festival. As the player who had appeared in more festival matches than any other, Gooch expressed the thanks of all the cricketers involved. He continued: 'The people of the north-east certainly supported you tremendously and showed to those of us within the game how passionately they want, no, deserve, first-class cricket in the region. I'm sure, when Durham achieve their "dream", they will look back on the Callers-Pegasus Cricket Festival as one of the major factors in their progress towards that goal.'

Brian Hunt's compilation of records from the ten years of the festival (page 37) gives an indication of the quality of players who were on view. Not only did they provide excellent entertainment and illustrate vividly that there was a place for top-class cricket in the north-east, but they helped to raise some £170,000 for cricket in the region.

Durham County Cricket Club matches against overseas tourists and the Callers-Pegasus Festival have not been the only events to bring first-class cricketers to the north-east. Durham University Cricket Club can boast an impressive roll of honour. In fact, in recent years, such has been the reputation of the university that, given the choice, some academically gifted cricketers have opted for Durham in preference to Oxford or Cambridge, and many have chosen Durham before other universities.

According to Dr Grenville Holland, president of the club, and in many ways its inspiration, cricket was first played at the university in 1843. A contemporary newspaper account, dated 9 June of that year, records a low-scoring encounter between the university and Sunderland on the Racecourse Ground. In two innings the students managed 80 (46 and

34); no match for the single-innings total of 84 made by the visitors. A week later, the university played Durham City in an even less distinguished game. The university made 28 and 12 to lose by an innings and 27 runs.

There seems little doubt that the founding fathers of Durham University Cricket Club were Joseph Waite and Charles Henry Ford. The first of these freshmen was to become Master of University College, while the other became Rector of Sedgefield and served that parish for many years.

In 1843 the Racecourse Ground was owned by the Bishop of Chester, a canon of the cathedral, and in 1844 Durham City Cricket Club took a lease on the ground from the Bishop. The lease and the associated estate passed to the university in the late 1840s but the city club continued to play there until 1887, when it moved, amid mutterings of discontent, to its present home. In the same year, racing was also brought to a halt by the university authorities – a source of further friction with the city – and in 1888 Durham University Cricket Club took possession of the Racecourse Ground and began a programme of regular fixtures that has continued until the present day.

The UAU (Universities Athletic Union) Championship, competed for annually by the universities, was founded in 1927 and became an integral part of that fixture list. Durham's name was not engraved on the trophy until 1938, and again in 1939. One of the leading players at that time was Syd Holgate, who was later to become Registrar of Durham University and Master of Grey College.

The university's next successful campaign was not until 1953, and there is no doubt about the identity of the leading player that season. Within a year, Frank Tyson was terrorising the Australians to such an extent that the 1954–55 Ashes series will always be remembered as his. One can only imagine the effect he had on opposing undergraduates in 1953. Tyson was twenty-three years of age then, and is unlikely to have been much slower than when at his peak. Indeed, he states in his autobiography that he was as quick as ever during his time at Durham. He also wrote that 'the university side was a most accomplished one and included players from three minor counties, one Indian State and several good league clubs. I honestly think it was a side that could have extended an average Oxford or Cambridge team.' It is an argument that has come to the fore again in recent years.

In 1972, the UAU Championship was secured again, as Durham University Cricket Club entered a phase in its history studded with success. Since and including that 1972 victory, Durham have been champions eight times. In the period 1984 to 1991 they were in every final, winning four and losing four. This means they lost only four UAU matches in eight years, at a time when the 2nd XI, more often than not, were also winning their competition.

This record of success and quality has been another significant reason for the focus of attention on cricket in the north-east. The level of regional awareness about the game has been raised by the publicity surrounding Durham University cricket. That publicity peaked in 1989 when the Combined Universities side reached the quarter-finals of the Benson & Hedges Cup, and came within three runs of claiming a semi-final place. No fewer than five members of that side came from Durham University.

Before 1987, the Combined Universities had been the domain of Oxford and Cambridge. Victories against first-class counties were as common as hens' teeth. Then the format was widened to include other universities, and the first-class counties ceased to regard the presence of the students on the cup fixture card as an automatic four points.

The new era began with a match against Surrey at Fenner's. The Universities were bowled out for only 116, with the three top scorers in the innings – Martin Speight, Nasser Hussain and Jon Longley – all coming from Durham. Surrey were then restricted to 107 for 9 in their allotted overs, with an off-spinner on Surrey's books, James Boiling, winning the individual award for bowling figures of 8-3-9-3. He also came from Durham University. In the next match, Middlesex inflicted a resounding defeat by 8 wickets, but then came a meeting with Worcestershire.

The Durham contingent was raised to five, with Tim O'Gorman joining the four who had done so well against Surrey. He did not feature with the bat, but held two catches, as did wicket-keeper Martin Speight. The Worcestershire side at that time was perhaps the most feared in the land in one-day cricket and included six Test players. Their innings was opened by Tim Curtis and Gordon Lord – both former students at Durham University. A total of 216 for 8 in 55 overs appeared ample, but with Nasser Hussain top-scoring for the Universities with 67, the target was achieved with 5 wickets and 11 balls to spare.

There followed a 3-wicket defeat by Gloucestershire, off the penultimate ball of the match, but the Universities still qualified for the quarter-finals. By virtue of a faster scoring rate than Middlesex in the group matches, they became the first non-County Championship side to get through to the knock-out stage of the competition.

Taunton was the venue for the quarter-final and Somerset the opposition. Before it took place, however, all media attention was focused on the students, and particularly those from Durham. Newspaper reporters arrived to write features and take photographs; television crews could be found by the nets at the Racecourse Ground, in the libraries and following the new 'stars' around the city. Those in the cricketing world who had previously been unaware of the strength of the game at Durham University had no excuse for ignorance now.

Came the day itself, and the Combined Universities put up a valiant performance in defeat. Michael Atherton, captaining the Universities, put Somerset in to bat and saw Roebuck and Cook score 109 for the first wicket. From that sound start, Somerset moved on to 252 for 6 in their 55 overs. Boiling bowled tidily, conceding only 28 runs from 11 overs. Atherton took 4 for 22 with his leg-breaks, but the feature of the Somerset innings was the spectacularly good out-fielding of the students.

Wisden, which can usually be relied upon to give a dispassionate account, said the following about the students' reply, which centred on two Durham players: 'The Universities . . . seemed out of contention with 144 needed from the final 22 overs. However, a magnificent partnership of 114 in seventeen overs between the brilliant Hussain (118 from 145 balls with 11 fours) and Longley (49 from 39 balls) made victory seem a formality. Instead Jones came back with two wickets in an over, a run out followed, and the final over arrived at 244 for 6, with 9 runs needed. Roebuck had Tolley stumped, Crawley, who had retired hurt because of a hand injury, was run out, Hussain was caught on the boundary, and Somerset won amid tremendous excitement. Hussain and Speight had been allowed by their university, Durham, to take one of their final examinations a day early so they could play in the match, but Cambridge were not so accommodating in the case of S.P. James, who had to be replaced by O'Gorman.'

That final sentence speaks volumes about a subject that still arouses passion. In 1978 Cambridge University had allowed Alistair Hignell to postpone his examinations until after a rugby tour of Australia. Ten years later, another rugby player, Mike Hall, was given permission to tour New Zealand with Wales. He was reading Land Economy, the same as cricketer Stephen James – but James was given no such dispensation and had to miss the cup game against Somerset.

Meanwhile, in Durham, arrangements were being made for Nasser Hussain to take his final Natural Sciences practical examination two days after the Benson & Hedges match. Speight took his final Greek History paper the day before. The pair were then chaperoned by college bursar Edward Wood to prevent them from making contact with any student taking similar examinations on the appointed day. While the Cambridge examiners were accused of petty bureaucracy, those in Durham were applauded for displaying common sense and a sound appreciation of priorities.

A similar clash of interests occurred in 1992, when Philip Weston was selected to captain the Young England side to tour Pakistan. He asked Keble College, Oxford, for leave to go on the trip, only to be told he had to choose between his studies and his cricket. He chose to find another venue for his academic career and went to Pakistan.

Jeremy Snape was another Young England tourist. He was at Durham University, asked for leave to tour and it was granted. The irony is that Philip Weston was born in Durham and is the son of Mike Weston, one of the men credited with first proposing that Durham County Cricket Club should apply for first-class status.

Durham's actions reflect the philosophy Dr Grenville Holland adopts regarding a university education. He maintains that universities should be centres of excellence; that excellence must be reflected in academic standards, but equally in other aspects of life as well. He, and the Durham University authorities, believe that to attract a top sportsman, musician, artist or thespian enhances the overall quality of university life. All students must attain the required academic standards, but then other considerations are taken into account. 'Employers employ people, not degrees,' is a favourite saying of Dr Holland.

No more than an enthusiastic club cricketer himself, he was asked to become president of the university cricket club in 1971. He had arrived at Durham in 1965 on a two-year contract, which was later converted into a lectureship, and had always shown an interest in university cricket. He accepted the presidency on the understanding that he would take an active part in the club's affairs – he had no interest in being a mere figurehead. He has been vital in providing continuity to a club that can only hold its playing membership for three years at a time.

Grenville Holland rejects the idea that he is in the business of recruiting promising schoolboy cricketers at a time when Oxford and Cambridge spurn them. He is not an admissions tutor and cannot interfere with the admissions process, whose prerequisite is a high academic standard. At the same time, the lecturer in Geological Sciences has gone to great lengths to create the sort of environment that will appeal to good cricketers. Over the years, a tradition has been established. Good players initially set the standard, better players raised it, and even better ones came forward to combine their cricket and studies at Durham.

Once there, they are encouraged to develop their ability and mature as individuals away from the pressures that so often have an adverse effect on players of similar potential at 'Oxbridge'. While the latter are thrust into a limelight of expectation by playing first-class cricket – in most cases before they are ready – Durham's cricketers can go at their own pace. They play other universities, the minor counties, and even one-day matches against first-class opposition. They have excellent facilities at the Racecourse Ground, receive good coaching and adopt first-class practices without being exposed to demoralising defeats. Durham is, in many respects, just like any other university, but it sets standards that ensure it does better than most others.

Those practices and standards are partly responsible for the way Durham University cricketers invariably make the transition to the first-class game so smoothly. They take a very positive approach to the game and do things properly. Grenville Holland believes that even graduates who go on to play Test cricket look back to their days at Durham and appreciate the grounding they were given there.

The legacy of the camaraderie within the university cricket club can be felt long after student days. A newcomer to the first-class game who studied at Durham may well find an established player who also went there coming up to him for a quiet word of help and encouragement. It is a logical extension of the family atmosphere Dr Holland seeks to engender. He was delighted, for example, when former Durham student Simon Hughes returned to play for Durham County Cricket Club after a successful career with Middlesex. (Hughes happens to be godfather to Grenville Holland's youngest son.)

Although, of course, not all Dr Holland's cricketing graduates go on to play the first-class game, at whatever level they perform they often do so with distinction. Two Durham members of the successful UAU side of 1972 – Rod Dethridge and Brian Evans – played Minor Counties cricket with such distinction that they won man-of-the-match awards in the NatWest Trophy against first-class opposition. Dethridge won his in 1982, playing for Bedfordshire against Somerset. (Another member of that

Bedfordshire side was Mike Gear, who was to become Durham County Cricket Club's first chief executive.) Brian Evans represented Hertfordshire and won his award in 1984, also against Somerset.

Durham University students who have, in recent times, gone on to play first-class cricket include:

Paul Allott	Lancashire and England
James Boiling	Surrey
Colin Cook	Middlesex
Graham Cowdrey	Kent
Tim Curtis	Worcestershire & England
Shiraz Dharsi	Railways (Pakistan)
Robin Dyer	Warwickshire
Nigel Fenton	Cambridge University
Alan Fordham	Northamptonshire
Graeme Fowler	Lancashire & England
Mark Frost	Surrey & Glamorgan
Tony Good	Lancashire
Jeremy Hallett	Somerset
Chris Hawkes	Leicestershire
Stephen Henderson	Worcestershire & Glamorgan
Simon Hughes	Middlesex & Durham
Nasser Hussain	Essex & England
Jon Longley	Kent
Gordon Lord	Warwickshire & Worcestershire
Gehan Mendis	Sussex & Lancashire
Colin Metson	Middlesex & Glamorgan
Tim O'Gorman	Derbyshire
Ashok Patel	Middlesex
Martin Speight	Sussex
John Stephenson	Essex & England
Richard Swan	Scotland
Keith Tomlins	Middlesex & Gloucestershire

The list makes impressive reading. It shows the part the university played in putting Durham on the cricketing map and easing the county into the sphere of first-class cricket.

3

A First-Class Idea

The minutes of the Durham County Cricket Club committee meeting held at the Durham City Cricket Club on Monday 5 December 1988 read as follows:

Item 7: Other Business
The Chairman outlined the discussions which had been held on an informal basis with a group which was interested in the idea of Durham County forming a first-class side. Michael Weston gave details of the background to these discussions which, it was suggested, were taking place at a most opportune time. Following a discussion it was agreed the Durham County Club should look on this move in a supportive way, and to this end a sub-committee consisting of the following was formed to monitor progress: A.W. Austin, J. Iley, T. Moffat, S.G.C. Stoker, J.D. Robson, R. Jackson.

The discussions referred to had been initiated by Matt Roseberry and had been held on a couple of previous occasions. The reference to the 'most opportune time' at which the discussions were taking place was the result of impressions Jackie Hampshire had gained while at Lord's. As a first-class cricket umpire, he had his ear to the ground in London; and as winter coach at the McEwans Indoor

Cricket Centre at Houghton-le-Spring, he had Durham's interests at heart. He felt the Test and County Cricket Board (TCCB) might be open to the idea of an eighteenth first-class county, and suggested that if Durham wanted to fill that berth they should put the wheels in motion then.

If 5 December 1988 at 7.20 p.m. was officially the start of the campaign, the seed of an idea had been germinating for something like a decade. It appears almost inevitable that some such thought should have existed. Over the years, Durham had become established as a leading minor county and had attracted great publicity from exploits in the Gillette Cup/NatWest Trophy. Every now and then, a cricket journalist, faced with a blank sheet of paper and a looming deadline, would consider the desirability and practicality of introducing an eighteenth county to the sphere of first-class cricket. In themselves, such articles were meaningless, but they did ensure a continued circulation of the idea.

Given that, still vague, idea and the fact that Durham represented, arguably, the best of Minor Counties cricket, there was a compelling logic in suggesting that they might one day become that new first-class county. Not that logic had the primary role in Durham's initial discussions. Their approach was based on the dubious precept that there is no smoke without fire. In this case, the smoke merely served to obscure the odd spark that would eventually burst into blazing flame. If the fires of first-class ambition were not seen to be burning brightly in Durham, the authorities in the game would have no reason to sound the alarm.

Cricket has always tended towards the conservative approach. It has evolved passively instead of being actively developed. It reacts to circumstances rather than anticipating them. Undoubtedly, that is part of its essential charm. Hence, laws are introduced or altered only when common sense dictates that regulation is necessary. Changes to the structure only occur when the existing provisions cannot cope with the demands placed upon them.

It was really in 1895 that the County Championship as we know it took on a recognisable form. Unofficial champions had been declared since 1864, and the first signs of the competition's being formally regulated came in 1873. The counties involved at that time were Derbyshire, Gloucestershire, Kent, Lancashire, Middlesex, Nottinghamshire, Surrey, Sussex and Yorkshire. In 1891 Derbyshire were excluded from the competition because they had won only one match in four years, and Somerset took their place in the somewhat erratic scheme of things.

The championship, however, was organised and regulated by county officials from 1895. In that year, Derbyshire were re-admitted to the select company, and Essex, Hampshire, Leicestershire and Warwickshire were included for the first time. Durham, along with the other minor counties, were left to contemplate their fate as a second-class club.

Worcestershire, having shared the first Minor Counties Championship in 1895 with Durham and Norfolk, and won the next three outright, were admitted to the fold in 1899. Northamptonshire shared the Minor Counties title with Buckinghamshire in 1899, with Durham and Glamorgan in 1900, had clear wins in 1903 and 1904, and in 1905 became the sixteenth first-class county. Glamorgan made up the number to seventeen in 1921. The precedents were, therefore, somewhat distant when Durham applied for first-class status some seventy years later. It had been enough in 1921 for the Marylebone Cricket Club to suggest to the Welsh county that there was space for another name on the first-class list and that they appeared to fit the bill. They were required to arrange and fulfil eight home and eight away fixtures against existing first-class counties. That done, Glamorgan became the seventeenth side to compete in the County Championship.

In the same year, approaches were made to Buckinghamshire to increase the number to eighteen. Buckinghamshire, however, declined the invitation on the basis that they lacked the necessary grounds and resources, and seventeen remained the complement until 1992. It was not, assuredly, an ideal number upon which to base any sort of league competition, but if there were seventeen first-class counties when the evolution of the game turned in new directions, then seventeen they were bound to remain until there was a very good reason to change.

A decade ago, there was a strong suggestion that such a reason might materialise.

Norman Graham had enjoyed an admirable career as a seam bowler with Kent. At six feet seven-and-a-half inches in height, Norman Graham could make things happen if he got on a wicket that was in any way receptive. When he returned to his native Northumberland at the end of his career, it appeared that he might just have found suitable conditions for his great crusade – for Norman Graham wanted to take first-class cricket home with him.

It took some time before his initiative garnered enough attention to be taken seriously. He moved back to Northumberland in 1978, and it was not until 1983 that there was a real possibility of definite action. At the same time, Shropshire were also examining the possibility of an elevation in status. However, neither county went further than putting in a provisional application; they were merely testing the water.

For Norman Graham, it was not just a matter of taking a county up a step in cricket's hierarchy. He had the idea of creating what would have been a wholly new county club.

His plan was to leave both Northumberland and Durham in the domain of Minor Counties cricket, but to promote Northumbria as a first-class team. It was an interesting possibility, and in many ways would have provided for an ideal pyramid system of progression for local players. With a strong league system operating in the region, the best players would graduate to the minor-county sides. The very best would then have the opportunity to play first-class cricket locally, without having to move to another part of the country to fulfil that ambition.

If you were to sit down with a blank piece of paper and try to design the perfect structure for county cricket, you might come up with something close to what Graham envisaged for Northumbria. As it is, the new concept of Durham County Cricket Club reflects much of the thinking from 1983. Durham will be at the forefront of cricket in the region, with Minor Counties cricket promoted by Northumberland and Cumberland. They, in turn, will provide representative cricket for the best players in the leagues. Throughout the deliberations, negotiations and planning, much value has been placed on the notion of the new Durham being the representatives of the north-eastern region and not confined to county boundaries.

Back in 1983, Norman Graham did not get quite the sympathetic response his enthusiasm and vision might have warranted, and which the later plans received. Both Northumbria and Shropshire were told by the TCCB to conduct feasibility studies before returning to Lord's with firm proposals. To reach that stage would have needed total backing from everybody concerned. It was not forthcoming, and the idea of cricket's eighteenth first-class county coming from the north-east was shelved.

Although nothing ever came of Graham's plans directly, they played their part in keeping north-eastern aspirations alive. They also demonstrated to anyone who doubted it that more than mere enthusiasm was required if such a project was going to succeed. Enthusiasm would always be the driving force, but its power would have to be harnessed to give other factors in a bid a reasonable chance of swaying the cricketing authorities.

In the early 1980s the time had not been quite right. Not every component of a successful campaign was at hand. To have attempted to push it through then could well have ended hopes of success in the foreseeable future. If nothing else, the initiative had revealed the obstacles to be overcome and how they might be negotiated. Conditions had to be right. The right people had to be in the right positions: people with the vision to see the possibilities, to appreciate the risks involved, and to go about the task with a determination to achieve the ultimate goal, whatever difficulties were placed in their path.

Conditions would not automatically become favourable, but Durham was fortunate in already possessing a number of advantages. There was the strength of cricket itself in the region. The powerful leagues existed but, unlike in some other areas of the country, they did so in harmony with the county's cricket administration. The Durham Cricket Association represented ninety-eight per cent of all the clubs in the county, operating in nine major leagues. A mere sample of names of professionals engaged by those clubs indicates the standard of cricket: Wasim Akram, Richie Richardson, Lance Cairns, Phil Simmons, Madan Lal, Mohinder Amarnath, Wasim Raja, John Bracewell, Ijaz Ahmed. Cricketers of that calibre do not play just anywhere, but they set the standard and lift team-mates and opponents alike to meet it.

The North Yorkshire and South Durham League had won the League Cricket Conference knock-out trophy, confirming the strength of club cricket in the region. The Durham Cricket Association played an active part in promoting the idea of achieving first-class status in this environment, and in turn received total support from its members for the plans that were coming into focus. That was of vital importance to the overall package, because without support from the clubs there would be no grounds on which to play until a new stadium became available. (The club grounds that are to be used have all staged Minor Counties matches, except the Racecourse Ground of Durham University, and that hosted the matches against Australia's Sheffield Shield holders Victoria in 1991.)

Unlike most other counties outside the first-class sphere, Durham could claim the benefits of a proper administrative focal point. If a county side is leading a wandering existence and the centre of administration is the honorary secretary's spare bedroom, there is little chance of cricket in a county having a natural home. Just outside Durham City, at Rainton Bridge, near Houghton-le-Spring, is the McEwans Indoor Cricket Centre. A splendid facility for cricket, it could also offer office accommodation as a county head-quarters until the promised Chester-le-Street development was ready to house it.

Mention has already been made of the north-east's appetite for sport. Just as in any other area, that appetite is all the more voracious when it is fed with success. Just at the time Durham County Cricket Club was surging ahead with plans laden with optimism, so other north-eastern sporting institutions were experiencing a trough in their fortunes. This was especially the case in soccer, where the region could claim not a single First Division side. It meant that all energies were drawn to the emerging cricket project and not dissipated among a number of sports.

While the pattern was falling into place within Durham

itself, cricket, too, was in a suitable condition for the project to succeed. The game's administrators were struggling to find the right formula for the County Championship. After so many years of its existence as a three-day competition there was pressure for an extension of matches to four days. From a cricketing point of view, it made sense. The objective of the TCCB was to produce a strong England side. This, it was argued, could best be achieved by making the premier competition more nearly reflect the conditions found in Test Matches. A four-day programme would, in theory, ease the transition for players from county to Test cricket. Furthermore, a reduction in the number of fixtures, from twenty-four three-day matches to sixteen four-day matches, would produce eight days' less championship cricket in the season.

The advantage of more time for rest and practice for the players, to say nothing of a neater, more logical format, was offset by a diametrically opposed argument concerning finance: less cricket would mean less income. It was not simply a case of eight days' gate money being lost, because the amounts involved can be so small as to be insignificant. More important would be the loss of commercial opportunity. If a team is not in action there can be no local sponsorship of the day's play, and no letting of corporate hospitality facilities. The adverse effect is magnified when counties travel around their territory, playing in festival weeks. With fewer home matches, not every festival could be maintained, and that could mean losing members and commercial sponsorship.

As so often in cricket, a compromise was agreed. Some fixtures would be played over four days and others over three. As a solution, it did little to bring the championship into line with the needs of cricket and cricketers in the late twentieth century. It was bad enough that counties played

Mike Gear, Chief Executive of Durham County Cricket Club.

Don Robson, Chairman of Durham County Cricket Club.

Durham Cricket Club playing Victoria at Durham University's Racecourse Ground.

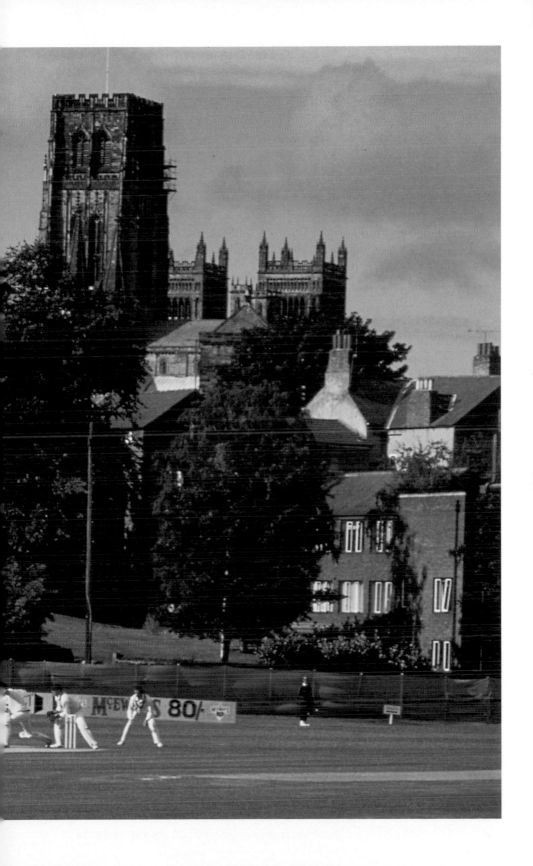

Geoff Cook, Durham County Cricket Club's Director of Cricket.

Durham County Cricket Club's crest.

The team's captain, David Graveney.

The site of the new County Cricket Ground at Chester-le-Street.

Ian Botham during Durham's first ever first-class league match, against
Lancashire, 19 April 1992.

some opponents twice a season and others only once. Now, there was the added anomaly of differing match durations. However, the compromise, by definition, went part of the way to satisfying both camps, though a powerful lobby still strongly favoured a move to an exclusively four-day system. That lobby might not have considered Durham's application directly in terms of an extra county providing more ammunition for the anti-three-day brigade. On the other hand, it was another point in Durham's favour. When it comes to breaking through a seventy-year-old barrier, anything that might ease the way has to be considered.

Similarly, the fact that Durham lies outside the boundaries of what was then the first-class map was a fortunate, yet important, factor. Had it been Berkshire making an application, situated as that county is in the heart of an area including Gloucestershire, Hampshire, Surrey and Middlesex, the outcome could have been different. There the new county would have been competing directly in the sphere of influence of other, established counties. Durham, on the other hand, were seen not as competing but as spreading the frontiers of first-class cricket to encompass new territory.

Events had conspired to create a climate in which Durham's approach could be found acceptable. The right people had to be brought together to fashion that approach in the best possible way. Durham were fortunate in that there were enough cricket-orientated businessmen on hand at the same time and in positions where they could influence the course of events.

There were men like Arthur Austin, former wicket-keeper, honorary secretary and then chairman of the club; Tom Moffat, another former wicket-keeper and then a committee member; and Mike Weston, a distinguished rugby international and an all-rounder for the county, with two top-class cricketing sons, Philip and Robin. Mike Weston's partner in the McEwans Indoor Centre project, Matt Roseberry, had similar cause for pride. His elder son, Michael, was capped by Middlesex as an opening batsman after appearing six times for Durham in 1984 and 1985; while younger son Andrew was on the Leicestershire staff. Then there was Bob Jackson, honorary secretary of the Durham Cricket Association at a time when it was crucial to have a man committed to the cause in that position.

One of the most significant figures in the whole campaign was Don Robson. He had been chairman of the Durham Cricket Association and in February 1991 became chairman of Durham County Cricket Club. He was also a long-standing chairman of the National Cricket Association and leader of Durham County Council. He had been a professional footballer with Doncaster and Gateshead in the League, and an enthusiastic if moderate club cricketer. Involved in business, with interests in sports shops and building, he is, in the very best traditions of the area, a good manipulator. Don Robson makes things happen.

His background was ideal to make things happen for Durham. His experience of National Cricket Association affairs meant he was no stranger in the corridors and committee rooms of Lord's. He could not necessarily pull strings but he did feel comfortable in the higher echelons of cricket administration. Similarly, his council work enabled him to find a way through the bureaucratic maze that a project of this nature was bound to encounter.

At the time of the application, the president of Durham County Cricket Club was Ian Caller. He had been involved with sport for many years and had a special interest in cricket through the company sponsorship of the Callers-Pegasus Festival. The family business was in the travel trade, and there was also a family cricket involvement. Ian's brother Roy was president of Northumberland County Cricket Club. To complete a family double, Ian Caller had received a call from Arthur Austin towards the end of 1988 to say that Durham would like him to consider becoming their president. He took up the post officially in March 1989 but was closely involved in the club's affairs virtually as soon as he had accepted the invitation.

Between that initial approach and his appointment, Ian Caller received another telephone call. He remembers that it was at exactly 11 a.m. on 11 November 1988 – seventy years to the minute after the end of the First World War. The call came from Matt Roseberry. He suggested that Durham should think about bringing first-class cricket to the region in response to public opinion, which was moving that way. Ian Caller realised that the first step had to be getting Durham County Cricket Club to sanction the idea; hence it was introduced through Matt Roseberry's business associate, Mike Weston, at that December meeting of the committee.

From this point on, things happened very quickly. A subcommittee of Don Robson, Ian Caller and Tom Moffat was set up to explore the possibilities and to draw up a business plan. Yet Don Robson had serious doubts whether a successful campaign was possible. Apart from the little matter of raising over a million pounds, they had to dislodge a century of history by changing a minor county into a totally professional first-class organisation.

Business experience had taught the three subcommittee members that the only way to succeed was to apply a professional approach to everything they did from the outset. Thus, accountants Price Waterhouse were asked to produce a business plan; a task they undertook with a thoroughness that set the standard for all that was to follow. If Durham were to advance their claim for a place among the elite, they had to show that they could meet exacting requirements of professionalism at every turn.

On 6 March 1989 a letter was sent to Lord's to inform the TCCB of the resolution regarding a first-class application passed at the previous evening's committee meeting. That letter was also a means of asking the TCCB what would be required of Durham before the fundamental step could be taken, and effectively enlisted their help in proceedings. The board's chief executive, A.C. (Alan) Smith, replied to the initial letter on 9 March, detailing how the Durham committee should go about securing its aim. In essence, the board would require certain assurances to be made and, providing that was done, the nineteen members of the board (the seventeen first-class counties, the MCC and the Minor Counties) would vote on the question.

After Durham's AGM, a special committee meeting was held on 21 March to review the situation, and produced a significant minute:

After discussion on the application for first-class status to be submitted to the TCCB it was agreed that, in the event of success of the application, the Committee is fully aware that it would denote the abandonment of Minor Counties cricket in Durham. On this basis a vote was taken for pursuit of the application to the Test and County Cricket Board – For 16
      Against 0
      Abstention 1

The committee had to decide at that stage whether to proceed with the application. They could have backed down, recognised that it had been a good but essentially impractical idea, and returned to pursue their minor-county interests. If they decided to go on, there was no turning back. The vote was conclusively in favour of proceeding.

Alan Smith suggested that he should pay a visit to Durham in May. If he had been in any doubt beforehand, he realised after his visit on 18 May that this was a serious proposition. People like Don Robson and Ian Caller were well known to the cricketing authorities. If they and Tom Moffat were involved in a project the chances were that it would be successful. Their standing in the north-east precluded them from being associated with a failure.

Surprise has often been expressed at the speed with which Durham's application for first-class status was formulated and accepted. It has been said that the game was not prepared for such a swift and incisive campaign. It was almost as if cricket was caught unawares by what amounted to a surprise attack on its stately portals. Nothing could have been further from the truth. The TCCB reacted positively to the proposal from the start and established a working party to investigate the matter. Durham were perhaps fortunate that one of the more enlightened and progressive of county chairmen, Chris Middleton of Derbyshire, was chosen to lead the TCCB's working party. He had with him the chairman of Kent's cricket committee, Jim Woodhouse, the chairman of Lancashire, Bob Bennett, and Steve Coverdale, the chief executive of Northamptonshire. Tony Brown, the TCCB's administrative secretary, took up secretarial duties.

The working party first met at Old Trafford on 15 September 1989. The matter was discussed and specific terms of reference established. In Newcastle in October, the group met the Durham representatives, who included David Pickford of Chester-le-Street District Council. At the heart of the plan was the construction of a new stadium, so the involvement of a representative of the local authority in whose area it was to be sited became crucial. The Durham contingent were already talking to other clubs about the way they operated. An approach to Hampshire, who were planning a new, purpose-built ground between Southampton and Portsmouth, as of obvious relevance in this respect.

The programme for Durham's application was determined by the TCCB, in that if they were to be playing first-class cricket in 1992 their bid had to be considered by the board's meeting in December 1990. Originally, there were discussions about the county appearing in the Second Eleven Championship in 1992 and in the County Championship itself from 1993. In some ways that would have been a logical progression, but what made good cricketing sense did not necessarily fit the marketing requirements. If the project was to succeed it had to have solid and immediate financial backing. The sponsors would be unlikely to provide money a whole year in advance of publicity returns. However well-intentioned the sponsorship was it had to meet commercial targets.

The TCCB working party appreciated this, and that they did so was typical of the relationship that developed between the Durham officials and the men whose 'club' they were seeking to join. Throughout the eighteen months of negotiation and consultation, Durham received nothing but support from the board committee appointed to vet their application. If the working party disagreed with a proposed course of action, they said so. They would, however, then put forward constructive proposals of their own so that the problem could be overcome in a way acceptable to all parties concerned.

The working party could not fail to be impressed by Durham's approach to a complex matter. The three men leading the bid presented a picture of total efficiency when it came to dealings with the TCCB. The business and marketing aspects were in good hands. What the working party could do was provide an insight into how best these business activities could be fashioned to suit the requirements of a first-class county cricket club.

Chris Middleton's committee met more than a dozen times before Durham's position was discussed by the Executive Committee and then by a full meeting of the TCCB. Six of these meetings were with Durham and six on their own. The board's accountant, Cliff Barker, was called in to examine the business plan with Price Waterhouse. Adjustments were made as the execution of the plan evolved. The TCCB's pitches consultant, Harry Brind, visited every ground on which Durham planned to play first-class cricket before the Chester-le-Street stadium became available. He gave advice and even listed equipment that should be purchased so that his advice could be followed.

The fact that Durham acted on all the advice given to them, and that the working party was seen to be on Durham's side, created mutual respect, and a close working relationship developed. It was a sensible and thorough way of going about things. While some people not privy to the inner workings of the game might, somewhat cynically, have believed that the purpose of the working party was to block the application, nothing was further from the truth. Encouragement was at the forefront of all their actions. So much so, that by the time the actual application was formulated, it went to Lord's with the full backing of the working party.

The bid had been carefully constructed along the lines determined by the working party, and, since it went before the TCCB with a recommendation that it be accepted, it would have taken a major upheaval for the application to be turned down at the crucial vote. However, the champagne had to remain on ice until 6 December 1990.

4

Marketing a Dream

One of the keys to the success of Durham's application was always going to be the marketing of the concept behind it. In the early days it was, indeed, no more than a concept, for there was nothing tangible to sell. There was no ground; there was not even a first-class county cricket club. The choice of organisation to market the dream of Durham as a first-class county would be crucial.

Don Robson had close contacts with a Newcastle public relations firm called Nova International. It was run by Brendan Foster, the former international athlete, who had been responsible for promoting the Gateshead Stadium and who was still a legendary figure in the north-east. Foster and Robson, who had been on the Tyne & Wear council at the time, worked closely on the Gateshead Stadium project. In October 1989, the two met again to discuss the marketing of Durham County Cricket Club. Robson explained the magnitude of the task to Foster, who considered all the problems, pitfalls and possibilities. Twenty-four hours later he called Robson to say, 'It's on; we can do it.'

Previously, there had been a few tentative attempts at fund-raising – the promise of £50 here and the pledge of £25 there. The first thing Brendan Foster did was to abandon that approach. As a form of fund-raising, it was perfect for collecting money to build a village hall. But they were talking about a project on a much larger scale and needed to go for the big money. Back in 1983, when the first serious enquiries about first-class status had been made by Norman Graham and his Northumbria consortium, the sums of money needed appeared as a definite stumbling block. Graham detailed the financial aspects in an article in *Wisden Cricket Monthly*, based on the possibility of joining the County Championship in 1987:

We would aim initially for a three-year platform. In the first season we would need £500,000 just to establish ourselves on a sound financial footing. Increased membership of, say, £25 per person, each summer could bring in £125,000. Sponsorship is vital. We could hope to attract one major local firm and various smaller concerns, giving us another £100,000. The TCCB shareout would be a further £60–70,000, with the rest coming from a number of commercial schemes such as lotteries and weekly draws, with any additional revenue from ground advertising. Once under way, the costs would be reduced, and we'd be looking at £500,000 over the next two years.

By 1989 the stakes had risen. The talk then was of one million pounds to get off the ground and the subsequent raising of half a million pounds a year for five years. It takes men of strong nerve and total professionalism, with the merest suggestion of being gamblers, to deal in those sorts of figures when cricket is under discussion. Durham had men with those qualities, and they set out to make the project work. If they could not raise the finance, the scheme could not be coaxed into the starting stalls, let alone reach the winning post.

Brendan Foster and another member of the Nova International staff, David Roberts, began to formulate a strategy that could raise the sums of money required. Strictly speaking, it was a business proposition with which they were dealing. In reality, the whole project became something of a crusade to further the sporting interests of the north-east, which were so dear to Brendan Foster's heart.

To gain maximum publicity for the launch of the bid, simultaneous press conferences were held in Newcastle and London. Brendan Foster fronted the north-eastern conference, and Don Robson undertook the role in London. Already people were talking about the idea. It now needed a big push to turn interest and enthusiasm into hard cash.

There might not have been a product to sell, but all the large companies in the region that were invited to send representatives to Durham County Hall on 10 January 1990 were left in no doubt that they had an opportunity to help make history. What had happened before had been preliminary skirmishing to prepare the ground; now the big guns were brought to bear and the push was on. If the mood had been misread or if this major presentation had not been pitched just right, the whole project could have foundered.

It is no exaggeration to say that the project was almost bankrupted by commissioning a video presentation to provide a graphic illustration of the county's plans. As it turned out, it was money well spent, for it opened the way to the sponsorship monies that were so necessary and gave a feeling of substance to what, at that stage, were no more than ambitious notions. The choice of personality to present the video was inspired. Tom Graveney, once admired for his elegant strokeplay, was still in the public eye as a respected television commentator. Furthermore, he had been born in the north-east, at Riding Mill, and if his accent was essentially a soft West Country burr, he could still summon up the passions of his Geordie origins.

'County Durham. From Tyne to Tees; from the moors to the coast its variety of scenery rivals any county in the land. In the time of St Cuthbert, whose resting place is Durham Cathedral, it was the centre of European civilisation. Today, it is experiencing a renaissance of the economic kind. Progress has always lived easily with tradition here; University College, Durham, is housed in a medieval castle. Now, Lumley Castle could witness sports history in the making. Durham is a first-class county in every way, except in one thing. In cricketing terms they are a minor county. The county club have plans to achieve first-class status, and those plans include the provision of a first-class ground and Test Match facilities on this lovely spot.'

While Tom Graveney spoke, the camera moved across the countryside and visited some of the famous landmarks. From Lumley Castle, at Chester-le-Street, it drew back to reveal Graveney standing on a mist-shrouded playing field. With the castle as a backdrop and the River Wear meandering around the periphery, it needed only a brief flight of the imagination to visualise a cricketing vista the equal of that at Worcester, where Tom Graveney had played so much of his cricket, with the cathedral towering behind.

Television footage from the Jesmond Festival punctuated interviews with personalities, both national and local, who added their weight to the cause. Tim Rice, as besotted with cricket as he is successful in the music world, commented on the enthusiasm for cricket to be found in the region and drew attention to the disgrace of having no first-class cricket north of Yorkshire. Record-breaking athlete Steve Cram made the point that once a top-class facility is put into a region, youngsters are given an incentive to improve in their chosen sport; interest is increased and there is a focal point around which to gather.

Steve Sutton from BBC North East referred to the number of first-class players brought up in the region who have had to go elsewhere to play first-class cricket. He felt it was essential to get a first-class county side in the area to keep those players at home. Steve Sutton's Tyne Tees Television counterpart, Roger Tames, is not from the north-east originally, but comes from Essex, where they know a thing or two about running a first-class county. He expressed the belief that Durham could sustain a first-class county team and pointed to the realism and ambition of their bid. Durham had needed a brand-new site for their headquarters and had gone out to find one.

Then it was back to Tom Graveney to spell out what Durham would have to do to secure the votes of the TCCB delegates. There were three main points on which the board would need convincing: facilities, talent and financial backing. With the clever use of computerised graphics, an artist's impression of the proposed new headquarters was superimposed over the field at Lumley Castle. There was a plan of the site with details of all the sporting and recreational facilities that would be available once the stadium and environs were ready, in 1995. Until then, club grounds would be used, and these were listed and described in glowing terms.

The next subject to be dealt with was playing talent. Durham's impressive Minor Counties record was quoted year by year, with special mention of the successes in the Gillette Cup and the NatWest Trophy. The man to talk about this aspect of the package was Neil Riddell – 'captain for the past nine seasons, he has been with Durham throughout the glory years'. Riddell willingly lent his support, dispelling any suspicion that there would be a serious conflict between the club players who would be deprived of Minor Counties cricket with Durham and those looking to grander horizons.

This had been a genuine concern in the area. Any county as successful as Durham would have a core of experienced players around whom the team was built. These players could be either too far advanced in their cricketing careers to be attractive propositions to the first-class county, or too successful in their careers outside cricket to welcome the uncertainties of full-time sport. Neil Riddell had made this very point at an early meeting when discussions about the application were taking place. He made it without malice or rancour, but felt it was his duty to do so. Of the side that played in the 1990 Minor Counties Championship, Riddell himself was 43, Steve Greensword was 46 and Peter Kippax 49. Greensword joined Northumberland for 1991, while for the likes of Riddell and Kippax the decision as to when to retire from Minor Counties cricket was made that little bit simpler.

Neil Riddell's appearance in the promotional video was a suitable seal of approval, from what might be termed 'the old school', for what was about to happen, as was a piece with Brian Lander. The captain of the side that had beaten Yorkshire in the Gillette Cup appeared as a National Cricket Association advanced coach to underline the depth of talent available in Durham. He mentioned that some 2,000 club cricketers turn out every week to play in County Durham; the strength of the leagues would be translated into a strong county side.

That system had developed players like Michael Roseberry, who had made such strides as a Middlesex opening batsman. Roseberry spoke in the video as one who had felt compelled to make the journey south to fulfil his cricketing ambitions. In future, he said, local cricketers could remain at home to reach the top in cricket – lads like Brendan McCreesh, a young opening batsman from Newton Aycliffe. He told of the youngsters who thronged the McEwans Centre coaching courses, their ability, and their hopes for the future of Durham as a first-class county.

The third leading requirement, finance, was dealt with by Tom Moffat, honorary treasurer of Durham County Cricket Club. He detailed the Price Waterhouse business plan, which would demonstrate the viability of the Riverside Stadium development. With known expenditure and anticipated income, he said, Durham should be self-financing by the time the stadium was in use, in 1995. Ian Caller reported that his soundings of both national and local organisations had been very positive. Here was an opportunity for business to participate in one of the most exciting developments in cricket for many years, which also gave companies the chance to help local lads represent their county at the highest level and then, possibly, go on to play for England as Durham cricketers.

To reinforce the feeling of a need for first-class cricket in Durham, chairman Arthur Austin recalled the days when he had kept wicket for the county in front of 26,000 spectators at Ashbrooke against the 1938 Australians, and another 20,000 in 1948. What better proof could there be that Durham people would support first-class cricket? Here was another testimony to the fact that it would find a natural home on the banks of the Wear.

'Business being business,' Tom Graveney's commentary continued, 'a company will expect some pretty solid benefits from their involvement with sport in general and cricket in particular.'

Brendan Foster was just the man to convince companies about the sort of return they could expect. Walking round the Gateshead track with Tom Graveney he recounted the start of that stadium project some fifteen years before, when those involved had a dream and little else: 'I see a perfect analogy with the cricket people. There are a few people in Durham County Cricket Club who have a dream, who have a mission, who believe this thing can happen, and if you look at the spin-off the region has taken from the athletics facility, not only for athletics but for the whole prestige of the community, for the identity of the community, for the spirit of the north-east, then I see exactly the same thing could happen when this cricket scheme happens.'

Don Robson was seen standing outside County Hall asking for the support of the region, and Brian Schofield from Cornhill Insurance recounted what benefits his company had garnered from sponsorship involvement with Test Matches in England. Speaking from Lord's, he gave an air of solid authority, which would appeal to businessmen – open their wallets rather than just pluck at their heart strings. Even so, there was still one more note to be played on those.

The video ended with young Brendan McCreesh striding out through a soft-focus haze to bat on the site of the new stadium. Tom Graveney gave an echo-laden commentary, imagining the day when a Test Match is staged in the Riverside Stadium and McCreesh of Durham opens the batting for England: 'He surveys the hostile field without a trace of nerves and coolly turns to face the West Indian attack. An ex-Durham schoolboy about to put his county and indeed the whole of the Great North-East firmly on the cricketing map.' With artistic licence at full throttle, McCreesh is seen playing the imaginary first ball for four with a copybook cover drive. A roar goes up from the crowd, the music swells, the credits roll, and the cheque books open.

The fact is, those cheque books did open. The video was

presented at 8.20 on the evening of 10 January, and within twenty-four hours Newcastle Building Society and British Gas had been signed as sponsors to the tune of £125,000. Newcastle Breweries were attracted as title sponsors. It would be their logo that appeared on the players' clothing and official documents. A national sponsor with interests in the area was less likely to disappear from the scene than a national sponsor without local roots. As sponsors of Newcastle United Football Club and the Newcastle Racecourse, the breweries already had firmly planted roots.

Experience from promoting the Great North Run had shown Nova the importance of establishing links with the sporting media. Thomson Newspapers had been involved with that enterprise, and the publicity thus generated played a significant part in its undoubted success. It was equally important that the media were involved early with Durham County Cricket Club's project. Consequently, the *Newcastle Evening Chronicle and Journal*, North East Press, North of England Newspapers and Tyne Tees Television all became members of the Foundation Fund.

This fund was to be the financial base from which Durham's bid was launched. With the video came a brochure outlining the opportunities available for corporate bodies wanting to support the bid and become involved with the new county club. In essence, there were to be three levels of corporate membership in 'Founder '90', with differing levels of investment and reward.

To gain the status of vice-president of Durham County Cricket Club, a corporate body had to make a long-term financial commitment to the club – £25,000 annually, for a minimum of five years. In return for one of the limited numbers of these options available, members of the vice-president tier of Founder '90 could expect season tickets and car-park passes, hospitality facilities, a match sponsorship and associated paraphernalia, badges, plaques, ties and commemorative photographs. Two ground advertising boards and scorecard advertising would also be made available, and the opportunity to use players for promotional purposes.

To become a corporate member of Founder '90, the outlay was a single payment of £10,000. This tier of membership was designed for medium-size companies, which would receive season tickets and VIP membership, plus a reduced package of peripheral benefits. Another category was added at a later date and called Corporate Plus Founder '90. This package grew out of demand for a midway point between corporate and vice-president membership.

For a one-off payment of £5,000, or £1,250 a year for five years, an individual or small company could become a member of Founder '90. One VIP membership, two Founders season tickets for life and some attractive trinkets were the lure, as well as the feeling of doing something of real value towards the fulfilment of the first-class dream. Like all the packages, it was available until the first ball was bowled in Durham's first first-class match.

Just as corporate involvement was designed to facilitate a broad appeal, so too was individual membership. No fewer than twenty-four rates for membership were introduced, with a ten per cent discount on all rates to existing members of Durham County Cricket Club who paid their 1992 subscriptions before 1 February that year. Basic full membership for 1992 cost £60; the top rate was £2,250 for life membership and spouse, and on a descending scale there were separate rates for country members, the disabled, students and, at the lowest level, junior country members, who paid a mere £7.50. To reinforce the idea of the club's regional identity, joint membership of Durham

and either Northumberland or Cumberland attracted a ten
per cent reduction on fees.

Adjustments had to be made to the business plan to
accommodate a balance between realistic levels of income,
while acknowledging existing levels of county membership.
Originally it had been envisaged that the basic membership
fee would be in the region of £100 a year. It was decided,
however, that it would be better to progress towards that
figure in stages. Hence it was proposed that the cost of
membership should begin at £60 and increase by £10 a year,
so that by 1996 – when the Chester-le-Street complex will be
fully operational – it would have reached the £100 figure.

As was typical of the entire project, there was no
shortage of ambition associated with the foundation and
membership packages. The big question centred on the
ability of these packages to attract adequate finance to
sustain the first-class bid. So, perhaps even those involved
were a little taken aback by the response. In a time
of economic recession, the way business and individual
cricket-lovers in the north-east responded to the appeal
was quite staggering. If the support Durham received for
what was still little more than a dream could be duplicated
in the existing seventeen first-class counties, cricket would
be in a much healthier state than it is.

Such was the promised backing that some announce-
ments had to be deferred until after the crucial TCCB
meeting, in case the jealousy of other counties was incurred.
Even within cricket, something of the patronising idea
persisted that impoverished country cousins should be
encouraged to make good. However, if those country
cousins turned out to be rather more opulent than the
family expected, a good deal of sympathy might evaporate.
Even after their bid had been approved, Durham had to
be careful about the way financial support came in. There

was the danger of a crippling tax liability if income was not carefully managed. This meant that some sponsorship was accepted in the form of services rather than cash, and property was purchased as a means of reducing the tax bill and to provide accommodation for players arriving from other parts of the country.

By 1992, sponsorship and membership schemes were working well. As well as the Newcastle Breweries main sponsorship, twelve organisations were involved in the Vice-President Founder '90 scheme. As well as the media organisations mentioned earlier, and the first two major sponsorships from British Gas and the Newcastle Building Society, there were deals with Cecil M. Yuill Ltd, Co-operative Bank, Durham County Council, Northumbrian Water, Rite Vent Ltd and Rothmans.

British Coal, English Estates North, Glaxo, James Burrell Ltd and Royal Mail had become Corporate Plus Founder '90 members. At the corporate level there had been contributions from H.J. Banks & Co. Ltd, Callers-Pegasus, Cooper Tools Ltd, Embleton of Durham Ltd, Mandata Ltd, George Mills Solicitors, Mono Containers, Tolent Construction and Tor Coatings.

At the next level down came Callaghan Price Accountants, Desoto Titanine, Dixon-Barker, GA Property Services, Gilesgate Properties, Harland & Co., Justsport, and Derek McVickers Ltd. Other sponsors, outside the Founder '90 scheme, included Archibalds, British Telecom, Compass Caravans, Durham City Council, Gateshead City Council, Sean L. Lee and Reebok. Not only did the money come in, so too did a variety of services offered by the sponsors. Whatever Durham County Cricket Club might need in the way of products or services to function efficiently, the chances were they could be provided by one of the sponsors. The county club and commerce in the region were entering a sound business relationship.

Membership figures kept pace with the growth in sponsorship. When the rates were published, the public responded by enlisting in large numbers. By the beginning of 1992, the number stood at 2,500. Judging by the rate at which applications were still coming in, it was quite conceivable that the 4,000 mark would be reached by the time the county began playing first-class cricket. It had always been expected that support would be forthcoming. Now, there was concrete proof that business and public alike not only wanted first-class cricket in the north-east, they were prepared to put their hands in their pockets to make sure it came.

With somewhere in the region of £1.7 million secured, Durham County Cricket Club could more than satisfy the financial requirement set out by the TCCB working party. They had the finance that would enable them to develop facilities while the playing strength was gathered. The formal application for first-class status could be made with confidence.

5

The Application

No one who was remotely interested in cricket and Durham's bid to become a first-class county could have remained unconvinced that this was a serious enterprise. In the winter and spring of 1990, a cricket fever gripped the region. The plan to involve the local media was working famously. Not a day seemed to pass without some mention of the bid. Admittedly, much of what was said was no more than speculation, and some of it was well wide of the mark. There was no danger, however, that the subject would escape notice and wither away through lack of interest.

As the county committee and the TCCB working party moved closer together, in what was becoming a common aim, so the bid gathered momentum and failure seemed to be no more than a remote possibility. Lest anyone failed to take it all seriously, the county published the details of its bid: twenty-one pages of text, diagrams and photographs in a glossy, colourful brochure that spelt out every aspect of the application. After a statement of intent, 'to provide a high-quality home for first-class county cricket in the north-east which will serve as a test bed for taking the game into the next century', it published the formal letter of application.

Mr Alan Smith
Chief Executive
Test and County Cricket Board

Dear Mr Smith,

This document outlines Durham County Cricket Club's formal application to the Test and County Cricket Board for first-class county status and subsequent eligibility to play in the County Championship and other first-class competitions from 1992.

As your board members may already know, our application is based around an ambitious yet highly realistic proposal to create the first new home for first-class cricket in this country for almost seventy years.

We see this as an opportunity – perhaps for cricket as a whole – to establish and develop cricket facilities capable of not only meeting the needs of the 1990s but of being flexible enough to meet the changing demands of the sport and leisure industry well into the next century.

May we assure you, sir, this application is not made lightly.

We enclose in support of our bid, certain information, plans and data which we believe clearly illustrates the depths of detailed consideration which has gone into its preparation, the degree of commitment among those responsible for it and the level of support which it enjoys.

You will perhaps excuse our immodesty if we also say it shows the standard and degree of support for the game of cricket in County Durham and – with an eye on the future – the strength in depth and keenness among all age groups.

Just as importantly, however, our submission also illustrates the short-term and long-term plans which form an essential part of our aim to be an asset to the first-class game from any date of acceptance.

We suggest it demonstrates our ability to satisfy the three criteria considered necessary for first-class status:–

(i) That we will have suitable facilities.

(ii) That we have the playing talent.

(iii)That we have the financial backing and organisation to both launch and sustain our place in the first-class game.

We also give you a firm undertaking to meet any additional requirements demanded of us to ensure that the county is as much credit to the first-class game as it has been for more than a century to Minor Counties cricket.

May we also assure you, again, if accepted, that we will operate strictly within Test and County Cricket Board rules and guidelines and in accordance with the spirit and ethics of the game.

In conclusion, sir, we believe we can bring much to the game of first-class cricket and that first-class cricket can bring much to County Durham and the north-east as a whole.

Accordingly, we ask that the Test and County Cricket Board consider and approve our application.

Yours sincerely,
A.W. Austin, Chairman
I.D. Caller, President

The application was lodged. It was endorsed in the brochure by the comments of a number of personalities and worthies who were keen to offer their support. These people came from cricket, from the north-east, or both. The combined effect reflected the breadth of support the application enjoyed, as mentioned in the formal letter.

Former England captain Mike Brearley wrote:
I'm delighted to add my support to the scheme to have Durham accepted as a first-class county cricket side.

Having played league cricket in the north-east for two seasons I am well aware of the tremendous enthusiasm for, and deep-seated knowledge of the game there.

There is a deep tradition of cricket in Durham, and the steady history of top-class players bred there.

The one drawback up to now has been the lack of sufficiently big and well-appointed grounds. The proposal for a new ground in Chester-le-Street removes that drawback.

I wish you every success in your application.

From cricket-loving author Leslie Thomas:
I was delighted when I heard there was a possibility that Durham County Cricket Club would soon be included in the first-class County Championship. During my visits to the north-east I have always been very aware of the tremendous support cricket has in that corner of England. I remember the two days at Jesmond a couple of years ago, when the ground was absolutely packed – despite the fact that on the first day there was no play at all due to heavy rain.

It will be these people who will support Durham County, and I wish them and you every success with your application.

My own county – Glamorgan – was the last to be admitted to the championship, and that was in 1921. It is high time there was a further addition. It can only be of great benefit to cricket in this country.

Colin Milburn contributed the following message before his untimely death:
I would definitely support Durham's bid to enter first-class cricket. It is a great sporting region, and compared to my

old county, Northants, of superior population and sporting tradition. Most county players who have played in the area enjoy the atmosphere and I have yet to speak to one who did not enjoy his first visit to the north-east.

The Roman Catholic Archbishop of Westminster, Basil Hume, wrote:
I would support very warmly Durham's application to become the eighteenth first-class county.

When I was in the north as a citizen as well as a schoolmaster, I realised how strong support was in Durham County. So I really do hope that the powers that be will add one more county to the championship, and especially so since there has been no addition since 1921.

Broadcaster Brian Johnston:
I am 100 per cent behind Durham's application for first-class status. The north-east has always been a cradle for quality cricketers, and I hope that the Durham County team will always include a lot of local talent.

Dr Grenville Holland, President of Durham University Cricket Club:
Our Racecourse Ground has been described as one of England's leading cricket nurseries. It is a cricket nursery, however, serving many counties, but not Durham. How much more satisfying it would be if we could continue to provide the counties of England with an ongoing supply of fresh talent as well as being able to sustain our home county with some of its playing potential. Cricket as a whole will benefit from this proposal. It is only by extending the boundaries of cricket, by embracing more players, administrators and spectators in an ever widening circle, that the game itself will thrive.

The case for granting Durham County Cricket Club

first-class status is overwhelming. I give my whole-hearted support and wish them every success in their endeavour.

Dacre Dunlop, Secretary of the Northern Council for Sport and Recreation:
The Sports Council and Northern Council for Sport and Recreation supports Durham County Cricket Club's bid for first-class county status and welcomes the development of a first-class county ground and associated facilities.

It is acknowledged that from a participant and spectator viewpoint the north has a fervour for cricket that to-date is not satisfied. It is our belief that should the bid be successful considerable benefit will accrue not only to Durham, but to the whole of the northern region. We also recognise that cricket will not be the only sport to benefit from the development as, through associated facilities, hockey, football and a series of minority sports may also gain considerably. The concept of promoting the new ground as a prototype for Cricket in the Community has undoubted attractions.

Former Durham University student and England fast bowler Frank Tyson:
It goes without saying that I wholeheartedly endorse your application for first-class status.

The reasons for my support, of course, take into consideration the enthusiastic support of the north-east for cricket and the potential financial backing of industry. But they transcend even these important factors.

For years I have been of the opinion that the north-east, Durham and Northumberland in particular, possess the cricket infrastructure which many English first-class counties lack, yet which is the very strength of teams such as Lancashire, Yorkshire, Warwickshire and Surrey. My own county of Northamptonshire, for instance, did not encompass the wealth of club and league cricket which lie within echoing appeal distance of Newcastle and Durham.

Not only are the Northumberland and the North Yorkshire and South Durham Leagues prolific nurseries of international talent, but they are inculcators of competitive attitudes, attracting good overseas professional players and coaches. Thinking back over the last forty years of north-eastern cricket, one can come up with a host of cricketing talent which the region has provided not only for first-class sides, but also England: Colin Milburn, Tom Graveney, Harold Stephenson, Dickie Spooner, Gus Williamson, and more recently the Roseberry lad from Durham School.

There are the players produced by the university: Simon Hughes, Paul Allott, Nasser Hussain and Graeme Fowler. I understand that there is now a facility which permits Durham University graduates to continue their higher studies and more advanced cricket in other older halls of learning. And who can forget the unexploited potential of players like Larry Liddell and Ken Earl?

The grounds in the north-east are of top-class standard and, in my experience, the administrators are of the highest calibre.

I personally feel that should your application be successful – as I am sure it will – Durham will soon find itself more financially and organisationally secure, and more able to draw upon a reservoir of youthful talent than other county clubs who have been members of the English first-class scene for many years.

My good wishes go with your application, which I commend most wholeheartedly.

Lord Elliott of Morpeth:
For most of my life, I have longed to see first-class cricket status given to the north-east of England and it is with maximum enthusiasm that I write to give my support to the application of Durham to become the eighteenth first-class county.

Sir Ron Dearing, Chairman of the Northern Development Company:
I wish this application all success because I believe it will add materially to the quality of life in the north of England, and thereby enhance our ability to attract investment to the north, not only in industry, but also in commerce, and in particular in hotels and tourism. I believe that tourism is a major potential source of employment and wealth for the north that has hitherto been little developed and that the creation of a club of first-class county status would be a welcome and significant element in increasing the attractions of the north for that purpose.

Broadcaster and former captain of Australia Richie Benaud:
The outstanding achievements of players over the years in Minor Counties cricket is a clear indication that modern cricketers will be able, successfully, to make the transition to the first-class game. The whole county, not just cricket, will receive a wonderful boost when the final decision is made.

The Test and County Cricket Board is not noted for its emotional response to the business of cricket. It is often accused of being run by accountants and marketing personnel rather than those who hold cricket dear. If, however, such a body was likely to be swayed by popular acclaim rather than purely financial considerations, the views expressed by such a diverse range of personalities could have done nothing but good for the Durham cause.

The brochure, very professionally designed and presented, drew on the success of sport generally in County Durham and the place cricket has occupied in that overall pattern. Even those who knew the area well should have found at least one or two facts that added to their knowledge. Anyone who was not aware of Durham's sporting traditions would have had their eyes opened wide. The first heading in this section read 'CRICKET IN COUNTY DURHAM – A SENIOR STATESMAN OF SPORT':

As part of the United Kingdom steeped for generations in the 'work hard – play hard' ethic, sport has played a central role in helping to weave the social fabric of County Durham and its inhabitants. Sporting tradition has bred sporting prowess across a wide spectrum of sports from soccer, cricket and rugby to ice hockey, boxing and even special athletics for the handicapped. Durham sportsmen and women have made and are continuing to make their mark at national and international level.

England's recent World Cup soccer manager and captain, Bobby Robson and Bryan Robson, are both Durham born and bred, and still have families living in the county, as has Spurs and England player, Paul Gascoigne.

Former Durham City, Durham County, England and Barbarians rugby union captain Mike Weston, later to become chairman of the England selectors, also played cricket at county level for Durham and is a current member of the Durham County Cricket Club Committee.

Football Association referees Pat Partridge and George Courtney have officiated at the highest levels of the game, including World Cup matches.

Olympic bronze medallist Charlie Spedding is recognised

as one of the country's top marathon runners.

Horsewoman Karen Straker of Teesdale, County Durham, won an equestrian silver medal in the Seoul Olympics.

Durham Wasps ice-hockey team are one of the premier teams in British ice-hockey, and have consistently produced players for the Great Britain team.

England rugby union captain Will Carling developed his flair for the game at Durham University, and his team-mate England fly-half Rob Andrew is a product of Barnard Castle School.

The list could go on.

Extend this extract from the county's sporting pedigree across the north-east as a whole and you have a region whose players, participants and spectators are renowned and respected in almost every field of sporting endeavour.

Given this sporting fervour, perhaps it is no surprise to find that:

– Durham hosts the country's second oldest regatta, dating back to 1834 and junior only to Royal Chester.

– Durham is the birthplace of the world's second-oldest soccer league – the Northern League – which was founded in the Three Tuns Hotel in Durham City in 1889.

– Durham County Cricket Club was founded in the same hotel some seven years earlier.

So then, county cricket in Durham is no youthful upstart. It has a long history and a proud tradition. But successful futures are not made by lingering on past glories. The bricks and mortar of Durham County Cricket Club's future success is the very strength of our game at all levels throughout the country.

How is this being achieved and sustained?

In a bid to generate early interest in all aspects of the game, Kwik Cricket was introduced within the last two years at junior schools throughout the county and the initiative continues to be supported financially and practically by the County Cricket Club.

The move proved extremely popular and has already paid early dividends. Just last year, 60 eight- and nine-year-olds at Pelton Junior School in County Durham became the first in the country to receive skill badges and certificates in the sport – whose regional organiser is also based in the county.

At a higher level, the coaching section of the Durham Cricket Association organises courses for all age groups, with particular emphasis on the development of young cricketers, and at venues throughout the country, including the McEwans Indoor Cricket Centre at Houghton-le-Spring, which is regarded as one of the best of its kind in the country and lies only a few minutes' drive away from the proposed Chester-le-Street stadium.

The popularity of the courses can be measured by their oversubscription every year, and the continuously expanding programme can only extend the range of opportunity to the young 'apostles' of the game. If the popularity of the courses can be measured in oversubscription, their value can be measured in the increasing strength of the representative teams drawn from the Durham County Schools Cricket Association – increasing strength which the results prove.

Whereas at one time a draw against Lancashire and Yorkshire was the best that could be hoped for, now County Durham youth teams are competing on equal terms, and in fact with reasonable expectations of victory.

The 1990 season's Durham County ESCA Under-15 XI – playing together as a team for the third successive year – remain unbeaten nationally at Under-13, Under-14, and Under-15 levels.

Their captain, Robin Weston, also led the England Under-15 XI during the season, and another Durham youngster, Keith Morris, was also in the National Under-15 team.

Two other young Durham cricketers, Robin's brother Philip Weston and Darren Blenkiron, continued the county's record of regularly fielding players in the North of England squads and national teams by playing in the England Under-17 XI.

Durham Schools have also hosted the National Under-19 Cricket Festival twice in the past five years.

Visiting teams have invariably commented favourably on the hospitality they receive from host clubs within the county and on the excellent standard of the grounds.

There is very close co-operation and a high degree of reciprocal support between the Durham Cricket Association, the Durham Schools Cricket Association, the Sports Council (Northern Region) and the Durham County Cricket Club.

Cash aid for youth cricket

The Durham County Cricket Youth Trust seeks to provide financial assistance to support youth cricket within County Durham.

Durham County Cricket Club was the initiator and is an annual contributor to the Trust Fund, which currently has well-invested capital of approximately £30,000.

Each year, every penny of interest it earns is spent on providing grants and other financial support to young players and youth teams within the county.

A difficult hurdle

The Durham County Schools Cricket Association supports Durham's bid for first-class county status.

After talking with colleagues within first-class counties,

its officials believe Durham youngsters are at a disadvant age when trying to break into the first-class game.

The cricketing infrastructure within a first-class county often affords better young players a natural progression into the county ground staff. Durham boys have a much more difficult road to travel to succeed.

One of the principal aims of Durham as a first-class county would be to create a focal point for the game at all levels throughout the north-east, and perhaps even into the Scottish Borders.

The vision of a regional Lord's, to which every cricketer could relate and aspire, would result in a physical home for the sport to which youngsters in particular could turn for help, advice and guidance, and use as a target for a career in the first-class game. By nurturing these close links with cricketers at an early age, Durham County Cricket Club would ensure a regular influx of talent to bolster its strength and ensure its competitiveness.

First-class status for Durham would be a great boost at every youth level of the game within the county and, as has happened with football through clubs like Newcastle and Sunderland, would increase the flow of young players into its highest ranks.

League structure fosters strength in depth

The Durham Cricket Association has a current membership of 117 clubs plus other affiliated organisations such as the Durham County Cricket Club and Durham Schools Cricket Association.

It is considered a strong and vigorous county association by the National Cricket Association at Lord's.

At its core are the ten leagues active within the county, most of which have 100 per cent membership (the least has 92 per cent).

More than 95 per cent of Durham Cricket Association registered clubs are involved in youth cricket.

It was obvious that this document was the result of a great deal of research and investigation. There is always a danger that such a piece of work undertaken by an outside agency will read a little blandly: technical errors creep in and the real substance of the subject is only glimpsed amid a welter of superficially attractive but essentially meaningless phrases. That was not the case with Durham's application document. It appears that every word was chosen for the precise effect it would have, and none missed its mark. After the extract quoted above it went on to mention Durham's outstanding record as a minor county, and the success brought to the county by the high quality of university cricket. It also contained an honours board, stating that eighty-six players from County Durham had gone on to play first-class cricket, with nine of them becoming Test cricketers.

Of the latter group, the earliest was A.E. Stoddart. Born at Westoe, South Shields, he went south to appear for Middlesex between 1885 and 1900. An outstanding all-round sportsman, he captained England at both cricket and rugby union. In all, he played in sixteen Tests of the cricketing variety as an elegant batsman, useful bowler and athletic fielder. Among a host of notable feats, he was the first Test captain to declare and the first to put the opposition in to bat. His ability as a rugby three-quarter won him ten caps.

Cecil Parkin was one of that not-too-exclusive band of cricketers to have played for Yorkshire having been born outside that county. He appeared just once in 1906 before it was discovered that he had been born at Eaglescliffe, just about the length of a cricket pitch to the Durham side of the county boundary. His subsequent career with Lancashire was interrupted by the First World War. He was at Old Trafford from 1914 until 1926, during which time his off-spin bowling caught the eye of the England selectors on ten occasions.

Roger Blunt was born in Durham but brought up in New Zealand, where he played for Canterbury and Otago. A highly successful all-rounder, he appeared in nine Test Matches for his adopted country between 1919 – when he appeared in New Zealand's very first Test side – and 1932. He toured England twice with New Zealand, in 1927 and 1931, and on both occasions played for New Zealand against the county of his birth.

David Townsend was, as has already been mentioned, the last man to represent England without having played for a first-class county. Born in Norton-on-Tees, he played in only thirty-seven first-class matches between 1933 and 1948, three of which were Tests in the West Indies on England's 1934–5 tour. He was selected for that trip as a result of his performances for Oxford University and returned to captain Durham with distinction.

Born at Stockton-on-Tees, Dick Spooner appeared for Durham before beginning a first-class career with Warwickshire at the age of twenty-nine. He was a wicket-keeper and left-handed opening batsman of the highest quality, but his England appearances were restricted by the presence of Godfrey Evans. Six of his seven Test caps came overseas. He played in all five Tests on the 1951–2 tour of India, and once in the West Indies in 1954. He made his home debut at the Oval against South Africa in 1955. Although not distinguishing himself with the bat and bagging a 'pair', he did not concede a single bye while 916 balls were bowled.

Jim McConnon, a tall off-break bowler and outstanding gully fielder, was born in Burnopfield and spent eleven years with Glamorgan. Just as Dick Spooner's opportunities with England were limited by Godfrey Evans, Jim McConnon was unfortunate in that his career coincided with that of Jim Laker. He did, however, get a chance in two Tests against Pakistan in 1954, and began his England career with figures of 3 for 19 from 13 overs and took four fine catches.

The next Durham-born cricketer to play for England also hailed from Burnopfield. The mighty Colin Milburn weighed in at eighteen stone and, at only just over five feet ten inches in height, did not have the look of an international cricketer. He was, however, a quite magnificent batsman, who would have undoubtedly reached even greater heights in the game had he not lost an eye in a motor accident. Colin Milburn was a great entertainer, on and off the field, and the idea of Durham becoming a first-class county would have brought a beaming grin to his cheerful countenance.

A contemporary of Milburn's at Northamptonshire was Peter Willey. There was a well-worn path from the north-east to Northampton, and Peter Willey followed it to make his county debut in 1966, when only sixteen years of age. He stayed there until 1983, and then moved to Leicestershire. Born in Sedgefield, he personified the image of the tough Geordie, catching the selectors' collective eye on twenty-six occasions, usually when they required someone who would stand firm in the face of exceptionally fast bowling.

Bob Willis was born in Sunderland but played his early first-class cricket with Surrey before moving on to captain Warwickshire. He also captained England, and was the spearhead of their attack for many years. He played in ninety Tests and captured 325 wickets with a wholehearted approach to bowling fast. Such a bowler was always liable to be prone to injury, and Bob Willis had more than his fair share of fitness problems. Perhaps it was his Wearside background that provided him with the courage to continue.

The brochure containing Durham's application for elevation to the first-class ranks included what were termed 'other well-known first-class players': Maurice Nichol (Worcestershire, 1928–34), Harold Stephenson (Somerset, 1948–64), Jackie Fox (Warwickshire, 1959–61), Alan Townsend (Warwickshire, 1948–60), Hugh Dales (Middlesex, 1920–30), Ossie Wheatley (Cambridge University, Warwickshire and Glamorgan, 1957–70), George Sharp (Northamptonshire, 1968–82), and Paul Romaines (Northamptonshire and Gloucestershire, 1975–90).

In addition to Peter Willey and Paul Romaines, the brochure pointed out that eight Durham-born players were contracted to first-class counties in the 1989 season. Michael Roseberry was with Middlesex and his brother Andrew with Leicestershire; Gareth Smith and Simon Brown were with Northamptonshire; Ian Smith was playing for Glamorgan; Andrew Robson was on Surrey's staff; and both Gareth Williamson and Graeme Welch were with Warwickshire. The point about the potential playing strength of Durham was convincingly made.

Within the application there was also extensive mention of the plans for the new ground at Chester-le-Street, along with details of other grounds on which first-class cricket would be played until the new stadium became available. This was an integral part of the plan, for not only were the TCCB paying a lot of attention to the Chester-le-Street development, they would also want to know how Durham intended to stage first-class cricket in the period leading up to its opening. The fact that there were adequate club grounds in County Durham with experience of staging matches, and which could be brought up to first-class standards, was important for the success of the whole proposal. So, too, was the fact that the county club enjoyed close relationships with, and the support of, those clubs.

The Chester-le-Street stadium also featured largely in the business plan. Under the heading 'THE WAY FORWARD: BUSINESS PLAN SUMMARY', the bare bones of the commercial and trading strategy were made plain for the members of the TCCB when they deliberated Durham's application:

The business plan for Durham County Cricket Club forms a key part of the club's application to the Test and County Cricket Board for first-class county status.

It spans a seven-year period from 1 January 1992, which, it has had to be assumed, will be the year in which first-class status is attained.

The plan demonstrates the club's recognition that a first-class county needs not only to be a cricket club, but also a financially viable business which needs to market its product and its services.

It achieves this by addressing in detail the key issues of management, finance, operations and marketing, and by outlining what Durham has to offer the first-class game.

Management
The club will be managed by a board of directors.

Key personnel will be appointed prior to 1992. These include a:
  – chief executive
  – commercial manager
  – team manager.

The chief executive will have had previous commercial experience at a senior level and will be committed to the success of Durham.

The club has already appointed former Northamptonshire and England player Mr Geoff Cook, Secretary of the Professional Cricketers' Association, to assist with the final stages of this application and to help plan and prepare for participation in the first-class game should it prove successful.

Finance

£500,000 start-up finance to be raised through a package of life and founder membership.

Major sponsor secured.

Adopting a prudent approach, the cricket club will begin to be profitable from 1992 onwards.

Operations

From 1992 to 1994 Durham will use high-quality local grounds.

In 1995, the new stadium will open.

The playing staff will include a high-quality overseas player and a mixture of experienced players and young local players.

Marketing

A marketing strategy has been developed which is aimed at:

    – establishing the credibility of Durham

    – responding to market trends

    – securing future business

    – providing a service all the year round

    – modern stadium management.

What Durham has to offer

A unique opportunity to extend the boundaries of first-class cricket.

A new purpose-built, showpiece stadium including a multi-purpose all-weather ground.

A source of quality players from the flourishing senior leagues, school cricket and well-organised junior leagues.

A stronger County Championship.

A new county will generate additional interest in county cricket, benefiting all counties.

The business plan has been prepared using realistic financial forecasts based on the latest annual accounts of all first-class county cricket clubs and TCCB accounts, coupled with several assumptions, including those of interest and inflation rates, the new stadium being available for use at the start of the 1995 season and, of course, that first-class status is attained in 1992.

The fact that Durham had been working so closely with the TCCB working party meant that the application had a better than average chance of receiving a favourable hearing. They had been working together to produce an acceptable format and, while there was still a chance that there would be a sudden change of heart by enough board members to cause problems, the indications were that Durham's bid would be approved.

Despite concerted efforts to get the bureaucratic tangle unravelled in time, planning consent for the stadium had not actually been secured by the time the TCCB's winter meeting took place on 5 and 6 December 1990. The discussion of the application took place on the day before to the official announcement, which was made at five o'clock on the evening of Thursday 6 December.

Don Robson, Arthur Austin and David Roberts of Nova International were in London to await the announcement. Ian Caller and the rest of the planning team were back home. All were confident of being accepted but steeled themselves to take nothing for granted. Don Robson had been given a hint on Wednesday evening that Thursday would be a good day for Durham. A member of the board passed him in a corridor of the Post House Hotel, Hampstead, and just said, 'Good luck in 1992.' Just down the road, at Lord's, that hint became a confirmation when TCCB chief executive Alan Smith and Peter Smith, the media manager, entered the press conference to announce the results of the board's deliberations at the two-day meeting.

It had been a unanimous decision – Durham would become a first-class county in 1992, providing certain requirements were met before 1 February 1991. Planning permission for the Chester-le-Street complex had to be confirmed; and a chief executive had to be appointed, as did a groundsman to oversee the development of the stadium and the preparation of the grounds that were to be used for first-class cricket until the stadium became available.

In Durham there were the expected scenes of celebration. In London, Don Robson felt drained. He, Arthur Austin and David Roberts shared a bottle of champagne on the train back home, but there was a feeling almost of anti-climax. They knew they had achieved the hard part of their campaign. The harder part now began.

6

Foundations for First-Class Cricket

One of the conditions for granting first-class status to Durham, the appointment of a chief executive, was achieved with a minimum of fuss. Having said that, this was always going to be a key appointment. Durham were, in many ways, breaking the accepted cricketing mould, so attitude and potential became almost more important than proven ability. In circumstances in which so much depended on ambition to build upon the exciting foundations, the need was for a visionary – a visionary, but not a dreamer. The man who got the job would have to be able to make the most of resources by his own hard work.

There were plenty of candidates for the post already established in similar positions in cricket, and applications arrived from men with outstanding records who would undoubtedly have done a fine job for Durham. The man chosen, however, had not been a county secretary or chief executive before. It was decided that, for a new venture, Durham wanted a man who could bring fresh ideas and not be restricted by accepted practices and approaches. In uncharted territory, it is the innovative who survive.

Mike Gear went to Durham with a sound cricketing pedigree and a long background in administration. He had played representative cricket for both Kent and London when at school and then gone on to teacher training college.

He spent three years at the Oval playing as an amateur with Surrey Second Eleven, and also appeared for Essex II while teaching in Basildon. He scored some runs but was not sure in his own mind that he was good enough to make a career out of playing cricket.

He was certainly good enough as a batsman to be a real force in the club game. He appeared for three of the best clubs in the south. Forest Hill, in south-east London, was among the very best, and could field a side that could have held its own in Minor Counties cricket. While he was playing for Tunbridge Wells, Mike Gear won the man-of-the-match award in the final of the national club knock-out competition. When he was playing for Cowley St John in Oxford, they won the league and provided a high proportion of the Oxfordshire side.

Gear appeared in two Minor Counties Championship sides while with Bedfordshire. He played for them between 1970 and 1982, helping them to take the title in his first year and again in 1972. He then had a couple of seasons with Buckinghamshire, scoring 49 in the 1983 Challenge Match against Hertfordshire, which Buckinghamshire just lost. He was chosen for the Minor Counties representative side in the Benson & Hedges Cup and toured Australia with the Club Cricket Conference, scoring over 500 runs at a good average.

He moved into cricket administration in 1981, when he was appointed assistant secretary (cricket) of the Test and County Cricket Board under Donald Carr. After nine years in that post he was seconded to the National Cricket Association to co-ordinate their Development of Excellence programme. He had applied for other vacancies with counties and had either not been selected or had decided that the conditions were not quite right. In Durham's case, everything appeared right from the outset. He knew and had worked with Don Robson on National Cricket Association matters, and appreciated the fact that he would start with a blank sheet of paper.

In fact, when Mike Gear arrived at the office of Durham County Cricket Club in the McEwans Centre in Houghton-le-Spring in April 1991, there was little more than a blank sheet of paper on which to work. His office, doubling as the boardroom, contained nothing but an imposing table. In years to come, when that table is suitably housed in the more luxurious surroundings of the Riverside Stadium in Chester-le-Street, it will be part of the fabric of Durham's history. Around that table were made the decisions that shaped the destiny of the club.

Mike Gear relied on the marvellous spirit of camaraderie that exists in cricket to garner instant experience. He enjoyed a close relationship with all the other counties through his work at Lord's, and now he used those contacts when help was needed. Competition between counties is fierce on the field. Off it, there is a strong bond of sympathy between them. It might be argued that such sentiments are born solely of commercial necessity; that there is enough outside pressure on cricket to demand co-operation between clubs in the interests of collective survival. Such might be the case in any number of professional sports, but there cannot be many in which so much warmth is associated with the spirit of common endeavour.

It might be thought that this spirit could have become slightly diluted with the arrival of Durham on the first-class scene. After all, with the TCCB cake being divided eighteen rather than seventeen ways, each slice would be proportionally smaller. There could have been outright disapproval, even resentment, from some of the less affluent counties at the thought of a new arrival grabbing so much publicity, and with it so many commercial benefits.

This did not happen. Mike Gear found all the other counties totally supportive. Instead of taking the attitude that Durham were depriving the established first-class counties of opportunities, the general mood was that they were bringing in new ones for cricket as a whole. With the advantage of not being weighed down by outmoded systems and practices, Durham could create those opportunities to develop a model operation, designed to function with total efficiency. The county could become the proving ground for many ideas that might, in the not-too-distant future, be copied by others.

To achieve the level of success required, there had to be an equally supportive attitude within the county. Cricket was part of the heritage of Durham, but based on the recreational game and organised on a voluntary basis. Now that game had been transplanted and had to grow in a totally professional environment. It was no longer enough to rely on the services of a volunteer tea lady, for example; professional caterers were needed. The club secretary could not be expected to put out boundary advertising boards and arrange the seating; professional contractors were essential. At the same time, it was important not to alienate the fund of goodwill that existed towards the new Durham County Cricket Club. Money can be borrowed or plundered; goodwill can only be earned, but like money, only too easily used up.

Durham had the potential to become as great a force in cricket as any county in the land. In order to realise that potential, professionalism had to be applied to every aspect of their activities. When you are dealing with millions of pounds, as opposed to petty cash, there have to be tight financial controls. On the field, there would be a professional team playing professional cricket. Off the field, Mike Gear saw his appointment as giving him the captaincy of an equally professional team, whose job it was to provide the very best environment in which the actual players could flourish.

The main difference between the on- and off-field sides is that the administrative team has its destiny largely in its own hands. There is no opposition, no form, no luck. Provided the administrative team is equal to the job in hand, there is no reason why suitable preparation for every conceivable eventuality should not guarantee results. This is the sort of preparedness a captain on the field strives for as well. His problem is the array of imponderables waiting to distort his carefully planned strategy; though cricket would be a tedious activity without them.

Mike Gear, ground administrator Joe Sherrington, and the rest of the team had an early indication that they were getting it right when Durham staged a one-day and a three-day game against the touring Victoria state side from Australia at the end of the 1991 season. The Victorians were in England to take part in the Britannic Assurance Challenge, in which the newly-crowned English County Champions would play the winners of the Sheffield Shield. Durham were given the chance to provide the Australians with their warm-up matches and to assess their own progress towards first-class organisation, both on and off the field.

Durham University's Racecourse Ground was the venue, and for four days the crowds were treated to what amounted to a festival of cricket to celebrate Durham's impending elevation. Rain affected the one-day game and the county were faced with a reduced target. Victoria, a team laced with Test players, made 232 for 3 in the 43 overs the weather allowed. Durham responded with 157 for 2 from 26 overs and one ball, to win on a faster scoring rate. Stewart Hutton with 55 and John Glendenen with an undefeated 69 paved the way, with an opening partnership of 126.

The three-day game that followed was not accorded first-class status, but was first-class in every other respect. Victoria amassed 402 for 5 declared in their first innings, with centuries coming from Ramshaw and Dean Jones, the latter against the side he was to join as overseas professional in the 1992 season. Durham, however, demonstrated that they could produce players of their own, with John Glendenen making 200 not out, as the home side reached 354 for 3 declared. Lehmann and Parker scored further centuries in Victoria's second innings, which was declared closed at 350 for 3, setting Durham the unlikely target of 399 to win. They were fighting to avoid defeat at the end, and reached 172 for 8 to secure a draw.

A win and a draw against the Australian champions was a thoroughly honourable result on the field of play. Off it, the administrative team had a resounding victory. Each member of that team was seen to do their job in a totally efficient and professional manner. Neither the Racecourse Ground nor Mike Gear had ever staged a match of that magnitude before, but the widely travelled and experienced journalist Richard Streeton, of *The Times*, paid them the ultimate compliment: 'It appeared as if you had been doing it for years.'

Comments like that go a long way to easing the fears and doubts that must exist, even when preparation is as thorough as it had been for the Victoria games. Proper planning had overcome inexperience, and it led the Durham team, with some justification, to believe they were ready for the big step coming in April 1992. According to Mike Gear, only one thing caused him undue concern about the 1992 season – he had no control over the weather.

The weather was also going to be a major preoccupation

of another new member of the Durham County Cricket Club staff. As well as a chief executive, the TCCB had stipulated that a groundsman had to be appointed. Tom Flintoft was recruited from Hampshire to fill that crucial role.

To a greater degree than in perhaps any other sport, the quality of a game of cricket depends on the standard and characteristics of the surface upon which it is played. As with the chief executive, Durham had to employ a man of the right personality and drive to ensure that they would encounter no problems with unacceptable pitches. However good the players they recruited, they would not be able to perform to the best of their ability if conditions were not right.

Tom Flintoft was no stranger to the region when he joined Durham. He originally came from a small village in Yorkshire called Fryup. He was a farm worker near Middlesbrough when he first became involved with cricket. Although never a player, he was asked to look after the ground of a small village club just to the south of Middlesbrough, at Nunthorpe. It was then that he started to become interested in the preparation of cricket squares, and eventually he took up a full-time post at Acklam Park, the home of Middlesbrough Cricket Club.

Once a year, Yorkshire played at Acklam Park, and with that background Tom Flintoft managed to secure the job of head groundsman of Hampshire County Cricket Club in 1986. Such was the quality of wickets he prepared at Southampton, that in 1990 he was named Groundsman of the Year for headquarters grounds.

When David Gower left Leicestershire at the end of the 1989 season, he decided to join Hampshire, and one of the reasons suggested for this move was the fine batting pitches he would find on the south coast. Tom Flintoft's award in

1990 gave substance to that suggestion, although David Gower, by his own lofty standards, did not quite do the pitches justice.

Not all Hampshire's home matches are played at their Southampton headquarters. The county covers a large area, and first-class cricket is also played at Portsmouth, Bournemouth and Basingstoke. Tom Flintoft had to supervise the preparation of pitches to first-class standard wherever Hampshire played. Such a task is not always straightforward when you are dealing with squares that are essentially club pitches, but it all helped make Flintoft the perfect candidate for his new job in Durham.

Until the new ground at Chester-le-Street is ready, he will have to supervise the preparation of club pitches just as he did in Hampshire. He is also in charge of the development of the cricket facilities at the Riverside Stadium, and he is helped in this by another parallel with his job in Hampshire. During his time at Southampton there were plans to sell off the County Ground in Northlands Road as a building site and move to a brand new ground just off the M27, to the east of Southampton. The scheme foundered well before Flintoft was able to begin work on the proposed site, but he had time to consider how he would tackle such a challenge.

When the opportunity arose to return to his home area and do what no other groundsman in first-class cricket has been able to do since Glamorgan moved to Sophia Gardens, Cardiff, in 1967 – namely work with a virgin field – he jumped at it. He would not be dictated to by what had gone before; he would be able to follow his own blueprint to develop what he regards as a 'good cricket wicket'. It is a term often bandied about in cricket circles, and can mean different things to different people. A good cricket wicket for a batsman is one with even bounce and enough pace for the ball to come on to the bat. A quick bowler's idea of a good wicket also involves pace and bounce, though not necessarily as consistent as that sought by a batsman. For a spinner, it will take turn, while the medium-pacer asks that it should be receptive to the seam, and so on.

Tom Flintoft's idea of a good cricket wicket is one on which the batsman can play his shots, confident that the ball will do nothing unexpected, while the bowlers still get a reward for the effort and skill they put in. Of course, captains and cricket committees will tell the groundsman what sort of pitch they want for a particular fixture. Most groundsmen are independent by nature. They will nod obediently when they are given their instructions, and proceed to prepare the very best wicket they can, while claiming it is exactly what was ordered.

If Tom Flintoft can produce a square at Riverside Stadium to meet his own criteria, the cricket played on it should be worth watching. The testing time will come in 1995, but as Durham began life as a first-class county, levelling work was just starting on the new square. Once laid, it will take two years to settle down and for the grass to become totally established, and then it should be ready for use.

There is no shortage of the latest machinery for doing the job, but when it comes down to it, it is the skill and experience of the groundsman that really count. Tom Flintoft found a local source for the soil he wanted. It was located in the grounds of Wynyard Hall, the home of Sir John Hall, chairman of Newcastle United Football Club. The composition of the soil used for a cricket square is crucial. There has to be just enough clay content to ensure that it will bind together but still allow adequate drainage. Sir John agreed to provide 1,000 tons of clay-based loam to create a Test-standard wicket at Chester-le-Street.

Until moving on to the new site, Tom Flintoft had to confine his activities to ensuring that the grounds to be used between 1992 and 1995 were of first-class quality. While each one is a fine ground in its own right, the pitches have to prove they can last for three or four days.

With the amount of league and cup cricket played on the best grounds, there is a problem for the groundsman in finding time to do the essential work. In this respect, the clubs were most accommodating in rearranging fixtures to give groundsmen adequate time to ensure that the pitches on which Durham played their first matches would be good ones. Even then, there was the perpetual imponderable of the weather. Tom Flintoft knew all about the climatic differences between Southampton and Durham. For one thing, there is a noticeable difference in the length of growing season. The cooler northern temperatures could present difficulties too, but the most serious meteorological factor is the cold north-easterly winds. They could dry out the grass on the surface and do more damage than even a sharp frost, especially in the spring.

The club grounds that were to be used until Chester-le-Street became available all met the strict standards imposed for first-class cricket. The brochure outlining Durham's application for first-class status contained details of all six grounds earmarked for County Championship and other first-team matches:

Darlington Cricket Club
Established: circa 1827.
Ground: Feethams, Darlington, County Durham.
League: North Yorkshire and South Durham.
Fixed seating capacity: 900.
Temporary seating capacity: 2,200 (folding seats).
Car parking: 120 spaces inside the ground, 400 externally.

The spacious Darlington cricket ground lies on the edge of Darlington town centre adjacent to Darlington Football Club's ground. The square can accommodate at least 20 wickets, and the ground has ample space for hospitality marquees.

The main East Coast line railway station lies within easy walking distance, as does the town's superb Dolphin Sports Centre.

Durham University Cricket Club

Established: circa 1835.

Ground: Racecourse, Durham City.

League: None. Teams contest the Commercial Union UAU Senior and Junior Championships.

Seating capacity: 1,000+.

Car parking: None inside the ground, but adjacent soccer pitch can provide up to 200 parking spaces; on-street parking and multi-storey car park within easy walking distance.

Superbly situated beside the River Wear and with Durham Cathedral and Castle as a backdrop, Durham University's spacious Racecourse Ground lies just a few minutes walk from the city centre. An excellent range of hotel accommodation is available within the city, and the town's rugby union, cricket and rowing clubs and swimming baths lie within a stone's throw of the ground.

Durham's railway station, on the main East Coast line, is two minutes drive away, and the A1(M) motorway is within a few minutes' driving distance.

Stockton Cricket Club

Established: 1816.

Ground: Grangefield Road, Stockton, Cleveland.

League: North Yorkshire and South Durham.

Fixed seating capacity: 880.

Temporary seating capacity: 2,000.

Car parking: 62 spaces inside the ground for players, officials and press. School, college and recreation field available for extra parking within 250 yards, plus ample on-street parking.

Stockton cricket ground is easily accessible by road via the A19, rail (Darlington station – 10 miles) and air (Teesside Airport – 15 miles).

Gateshead Fell Cricket Club
Established: 1878.
Ground: Eastwood Gardens, Gateshead, Tyne and Wear.
League: Durham Senior.
Fixed seating capacity: 400.
Temporary seating capacity: 3,500.
Car parking: 30 spaces available inside the ground for players and officials; 500 spaces outside the ground plus ample on-street parking in the vicinity.

Gateshead is no stranger to top-class sport and its superb athletics stadium has hosted many international meetings. Newcastle city centre, with its wide range of sporting and social facilities, is only a few minutes' drive away from the Gateshead Fell cricket ground, as is Gateshead's MetroCentre – Europe's largest indoor shopping and leisure complex. A wealth of excellent hotel facilities lies within easy reach; Newcastle Central station is only a few minutes' drive away, and Newcastle Airport is also within easy reach.

Hartlepool Cricket Club
Established: 1855.
Ground: Park Drive, Hartlepool, Cleveland.
League: North Yorkshire and South Durham.
Fixed seating capacity: 1,000.
Temporary seating capacity: 2,000.

Car parking: 80 spaces inside the ground; 1,000 in local schools adjacent to the ground.

The tree-lined Hartlepool ground can accommodate 14 wickets, and an area in its south-east corner has been previously used to accommodate a marquee for bar/hospitality purposes.

Easily accessible via the A19.

Chester-le-Street Cricket Club

Established: circa 1834.

Ground: Ropery Lane, Chester-le-Street, County Durham.

League: Durham Senior.

Permanent seating capacity: 3,200.

Total seating capacity: 4,000.

Car parking: Off-street car parking for 1,000+ within a few minutes' walk.

Chester-le-Street cricket ground lies just a few minutes' walk from the proposed new Durham County Cricket Club stadium. The main East Coast line railway station lies within half a mile and the A1(M) motorway is within one mile. A golf course, swimming baths, squash club and superb country hotel are all close at hand.

If the language used in the brochure smacked more of estate agency than cricket, it has to be remembered that the purpose was to sell the idea of first-class cricket in Durham. When it came to gathering votes, the chairmen of other counties would not be keen to send their players to an underdeveloped wasteland without suitable facilities. Any such misapprehension was dismissed immediately. Furthermore, by going outside the boundaries of County Durham itself for playing venues, the regional concept was reinforced.

These six grounds were only to serve as temporary homes

until the new stadium was completed and ready for cricket. This was the keystone of Durham's bid, for without the income from the stadium the business plan would not be viable. The TCCB working party realised this and so did Durham County Cricket Club. Not surprisingly, the application brochure went into some detail about plans for the new complex:

The way forward: ideas for Chester-le-Street Riverside

A site suitable for a new County Cricket Ground has been found at Chester-le-Street Riverside.

It is proposed to locate the new County Ground south of the picturesque Riverside Park and at the hub of a prestigious 43-hectare (107-acre) sports, leisure, nature conservation, office and executive housing development.

The landowners, Chester-le-Street District Council, have, with the advice of consultants, prepared an overall development scheme for the area and have recently applied for planning consent.

The details of the proposed development will take some time to prepare after the outline planning stage, though an illustrative scheme has been prepared by consultants which demonstrates the concept of improving leisure amenities in the area while at the same time, through developing housing and offices on a small part of the site, providing funds towards the cost of a cricket ground.

Development proposals for a County Cricket Ground at Chester-le-Street

The overall scheme includes the following elements:

Cricket ground: 7 hectares.

500 permanent car parking spaces for the cricket ground: 3 hectares.

Offices: 1 hectare.

Housing: 7.5 hectares.

Playing fields, athletics track, community sports facilities and 100 car parking spaces (provision for 2,500 temporary parking spaces on match days): 14 hectares.

Landscape and nature conservation: 10.5 hectares.

Total=43 hectares.

The proposed cricket ground therefore would sit in a landscaped recreation area which would, in itself, be a major enhancement of Chester-le-Street Riverside.

A NEW, PURPOSE-BUILT GROUND IS DESIRABLE ON TWO COUNTS

i. It will enable Durham County Cricket Club to bring something new to the County Championship in the form of the stadium itself and new ideas on how to promote cricket within the context of other leisure facilities.

ii. The new ground and promotional ideas will generate maximum support from a region where people are increasingly seeking to use their expanding leisure time in new ways.

CHESTER-LE-STREET RIVERSIDE: THE IDEAL LOCATION AND SETTING

Its accessibility from other parts of the country is virtually unparalleled. It is adjacent to a junction on the A1(M) motorway, within minutes of a main East Coast line railway station in Chester-le-Street itself, within 30 minutes' drive of Newcastle and Teesside airports, and within 40 minutes' driving time of 2.5 million people in Tyneside, Teesside, Wearside and County Durham.

THE MARKET

This catchment of 2.5 million people provides a market area with a strong and continuing tradition in a variety of sports.

The Riverside scheme affords a unique opportunity to

develop this market by providing first-class county cricket in the context of improving and enhancing the existing facilities for sport and recreation in the area, as well as providing high-quality housing, and offices to attract new investment.

THE CLIMATE

The Riverside is a relatively sheltered site with no more rain than Reading (which is on a similar longitude some 250 miles to the south) and more calm days than Bristol.

THE SETTING

The Riverside setting, next to the River Wear and sur-rounded by woodland, is overlooked by the majestic Lumley Castle and Chester-le-Street golf course. It is close to the historic town of Chester-le-Street itself, is outstandingly attractive and must be one of the best in the North.

The area is already associated with sport and leisure. A wide range of recreational facilities already exists on and around the site, including golf, boating, tennis, squash, swimming, soccer and rugby. Chester-le-Street Cricket Club's ground – already used for county matches – lies minutes' walk away.

If the language of the estate agent was still evident, so too was the language of the developer. Durham County Cricket Club might have enjoyed the support of influential men in positions of power, but they still needed actually to obtain planning permission for their ambitious scheme. In fact, it is not overstating the case to say that the entire project was balanced on, not the application for first-class status, but the planning application. Lord's had accepted the idea of Durham as a first-class county, but they had made that third condition – planning permission had to be obtained.

Any scheme of this magnitude was likely to encounter some opposition as it went through the various stages of official scrutiny. While the prospect of a new county ground might have been extraordinarily exciting for the cricketing community, there were inevitably some locals who did not greet the plans with quite the same euphoria. The planning authorities had to consider all views, including those of people Don Robson dismissed as 'the dog-walkers'.

The Riverside site was used for all sorts of outdoor pastimes. The reference to a 'nature conservation area' in the plans served a useful political function, as did the term 'community sports facilities', providing for the retention of the football pitches already to be found there. There was talk of 'professional' offices and 'executive housing', and celebrity naturalist David Bellamy was publicised as supporting the plans.

That the site was already used for recreation counted in its favour. As did the fact that few residences would really be affected by the development. The local authorities took the view that far more good would come to the area by accepting the Durham plans than would be achieved by rejecting them. However, there was still the possibility that the Department of the Environment might 'call in' the proposal for further discussion.

The TCCB had stated initially that Durham's application could not be considered unless planning consent had been granted. If the plans were called in by the DoE, Durham would not be able to resolve the matter in time for the December 1990 meeting of the TCCB which, in turn, was the deadline for the application's acceptance if it was to take effect for the 1992 season.

To add to the drama, discreet inquiries by a third party revealed that the DoE were loath to let the development plans go through unless Durham achieved first-class status. It had all the makings of a classic catch-22 situation. The full story of the dealings, discussions and negotiations that went on at this time may never come to light. More than one career and the whole future of cricket in Durham were at stake as an agreement was sought.

Fortunately, the matter was sensibly resolved. On 6 December the TCCB issued conditional acceptance of Durham's bid. Once that step had been taken, the DoE decided not to call in the plans and consent to proceed was granted. The official letter giving planning permission arrived on 14 December. The way to first-class status was now clear.

7

A First-Class Team

We have examined the business aspect of Durham's bid, the multi-million-pound development of the new ground, the marketing, the planning application, the politics, the finance and the commerce. It would be all too easy to talk about the transformation of Durham County Cricket Club in these terms and to forget that at the heart of the whole project was a cricket club. Cricket was the driving force and they were not going to get very far without a team worthy of the facilities that were being created.

The TCCB working party had highlighted three areas in which Durham should be able to satisfy them. Two of these were finance and facilities. The third was adequate playing strength. The application had succeeded partly because of the historical strength of Durham as a cricketing county. However, only a reckless romantic could have imagined that the Durham team for the initial first-class fixture would all be talking with Geordie accents. Having said that, Geoff Cook, the man charged with recruiting the players, did speak with an accent that was in no way out of place.

He was born in Middlesbrough, where his father was highly influential in local cricket circles. It might have been thought that such a promising young player would have been snapped up by Yorkshire, but instead Geoff

Cook followed the well-worn path from the north-east to Northamptonshire. He made his debut for them in 1971 and enjoyed a first-class career of the highest quality. To describe him, as so many did, as a thoroughly dependable right-handed opening batsman did less than justice to the wide array of attacking shots he possessed and frequently displayed.

They were seen at their best in the 1981 NatWest Trophy final at Lord's, when Northamptonshire were involved in a thrilling game against Derbyshire. Derbyshire won with a scrambled leg-bye off the very last ball, but only after Geoff Cook had played a marvellous innings of 111. It won him the man-of-the-match award and a place on England's tour to India and Sri Lanka the following winter. He made his international debut in Colombo at the end of that tour, in what was Sri Lanka's first official Test Match.

He came back to play in three of the following summer's Tests against India. He did a good job, scoring two 50s, and featured in opening partnerships worth 106 and 96 with Chris Tavaré. He had taken over the Northamptonshire captaincy in 1981, after doing the job with Eastern Province in South Africa for three winters. He was obviously well-suited to the role and, with his success as an opening batsman, was widely talked of as a future England captain.

That prospect diminished when he had a disappointing tour to Australia in 1982–3, and, in the event, he was not called on again by the England selectors in any capacity. He continued, however, to be one of the most consistent opening batsmen in county cricket, scoring over a thousand runs in a season no fewer than twelve times. Added to this was his occasional slow left-arm spin, his fearless short-leg fielding, and his thoughtful captaincy. Geoff Cook was the epitome of the good professional cricketer and it was a

Dean Jones.

Simon Brown.

Phil Berry.

Dean Jones.

Wayne Larkins.

Simon Hughes.

Steve McEwan.

Phil Bainbridge batting during Durham's league match against Lancashire in April 1992.

Ian Botham opening the batting against Lancashire. Durham went on to win by nine runs.

Durham's first league match was played on the University's Racecourse Ground and hosted by Durham County Cricket Club.

Paul Parker.

Wayne Larkins.

Spectators at Durham University's Racecourse Ground.

fitting tribute from his fellow professionals when he became chairman of the Cricketers' Association.

He ended his first-class career with more than 23,000 runs at an average of nearly 32, 15 rather expensive wickets, but over 400 catches. He had even found time to deputise behind the wicket on occasions, and had 3 stumpings to his credit. He skippered Northamptonshire between 1981 and 1988 and retired from first-class cricket after the 1990 season to take up his post as the cricket supremo with Durham. There were few men better qualified for the job and probably none with the same dedication, which he immediately demonstrated.

Cook was faced with three possible courses of action when it came to recruiting players for the 1992 Durham team. He could rely entirely on local talent from the leagues; which would mean Durham becoming the whipping boys of the County Championship for a few years at least, though such a side would be truly representative of the local community. On the other hand, he could ignore local players and scour the land for established professionals who might or might not have done reasonably well in competition, but who would give instant credibility and appeal to sponsors. However, they would tend to alienate partisan support.

The third, and obvious, course, and the one he chose, was to mix the two elements: use the best of the local talent, stiffened by established players from elsewhere, and top the mixture off with an overseas player of the very highest quality. Only time will tell whether this was a recipe for success, but it was an eminently pragmatic approach, as one would expect of a man like Geoff Cook.

Immediately it was known that Durham were to join the County Championship there was a flood of applications from players who wanted to be part of the team. If they had all been taken on, Durham would have been able to field four or five sides. Geoff Cook was not, however, merely looking for numbers. He wanted to be sure of certain qualities in prospective Durham players, as cricketers and as people, before contracts were offered.

His might have seemed an enviable task. In fact, it was not quite as simple as it appeared, and there were restrictions on his freedom of choice. Contractual ties prevented him from recruiting many of the players he might have liked to sign. Counties tend to be understandably protective towards the younger members of their playing staffs. It takes a lot of money and resources to bring a raw cricketer to the point where he is able to perform at the required level in first-team cricket. The last thing they want is to make that investment and then lose him to another county. At the same time, if counties are prepared to let a youngster move on after they have made that investment, one has to wonder whether he is ever going to be quite good enough.

Effectively, therefore, Durham's field of recruitment was restricted, as far as existing first-class players were concerned, to players who could be described as being in the final phases of their careers. Those Cook deemed suitable would still be ambitious and capable of a consistently high level of personal performance, but willing to fit into a team structure. They would be the sort of players who might have become just a little stale and whose careers would benefit from the stimulus of a new challenge. At the same time, their counties might be pleased to let them go so as to ease the burden of the wage bill and give youngsters of their own a chance.

Geoff Cook had not only to strike an acceptable balance between local and recruited talent but to make sure that the blend of youth and experience was right. Above all, he had to have depth in his first-team pool of players to provide cover for injuries and even Test calls, and to be competitive in whatever conditions they found themselves playing. As the build-up to the 1992 season intensified, he was confident that the twenty-two players he had finally chosen represented the balance he sought.

David Graveney was named as captain. He had shown in his captaincy of Gloucestershire that he had that priceless ability to make the most of the resources available to him. Almost anyone can be a good captain of a side bursting with talent. In truth, it takes an outstandingly bad captain not to win if he can call upon the best batsmen and best bowlers. A captain can be said to have got what it takes if his side's overall achievement is greater than the sum of its individual abilities.

Graveney had joined Gloucestershire essentially as a slow left-arm bowler and useful batsman. He made his debut in 1972 and four years later was awarded his county cap. Strangely enough, he was captain of Gloucestershire from 1981 until 1988 – exactly the period of Geoff Cook's leadership of Northamptonshire. There was another connection between them, in that Graveney served as treasurer of the Cricketers' Association.

Whereas Cook had resigned from the Northamptonshire captaincy without any obvious rancour, David Graveney's reign with Gloucestershire came to an unhappy conclusion when he was sacked. He therefore became the third member of his family to be dismissed by the county. His uncle, Tom, had similarly been stripped of the captaincy in 1960, while father Ken lost the chairmanship in 1982. David, to his credit, did not immediately leave the county he had done so much for, though the temptation to do so must have been enormous. Instead, he continued playing until 1991, when he moved to Somerset. He took another 55 first-class wickets in his one season at Taunton to add to the 829 he had taken for Gloucestershire, and showed that in the right conditions he could still be a match-winner, with a 7-wicket return in the first innings of Somerset's game with Kent.

He had often looked worthy of an England cap, but was not able to force his way past outstanding bowlers of the same type like Derek Underwood and Phil Edmonds. When the selectors did make serious inquiries about his availability, in 1988, he had to withdraw from consideration because he was not fully fit. He did have a taste of the international scene when he went to South Africa as player-manager of the unofficial and ill-fated England XI in 1989–90.

In David Graveney, Geoff Cook had chosen a man with a wealth of cricketing knowledge, who would play a crucial role on the field. He had exactly the character and experience to take on the arduous role in all its aspects. For the captain of Durham would also be a figure in the community, because Durham was to be a community club.

The other crucial appointment Cook had to make was that of overseas professional. It was generally considered that Durham's most pressing requirement was for a genuine world-class fast bowler; someone who could be the spearhead of their attack and give them a potent strike force. It was a fine theory; in practice, it was not quite so simple. Genuine world-class fast bowlers are not that numerous. Only a few bowlers fitted Durham's criteria, and they were already committed to other counties. Malcolm Marshall had been outstanding for Hampshire, and Allan Donald and Waqar Younis had done wonders for Warwickshire and Surrey, respectively. Apart from them, there were a number of fine bowlers who, though superb on their day, had not really given value for money and performed with the consistency Durham required. The men who did that tended to be batsmen, so the county decided to look for a top-quality batsman instead.

Through contacts in the Victorian Cricket Association in Australia it was learnt that Dean Jones was keen to play in English county cricket. It is commonly held that a player has not completed his cricketing education until he has sampled, and mastered, the variety of conditions found in the English game. Dean Jones had already sampled those conditions when on tour with Australia in 1989. He had topped the first-class batting averages with 1,500 runs at an average of nearly ninety, and had hit five centuries. He was also widely regarded as one of the best one-day batsmen in the world, and it was no secret that Durham's best chance of early first-class success was likely to be in the limited-overs competitions.

Dean Jones was a big name whose signing would have caused a stir wherever he had chosen to play. Having secured his services, Durham added another player to the squad who did not just cause a local stir – the reverberations went right round the cricketing world. He might not have been at the very peak of his powers, but Ian Botham was still one of the biggest names in cricket. He still had immense charisma and pulling power, and was still a very good cricketer.

Botham had matured as a player over the years. He had gone through the tearaway stage when a teenager with Somerset. He had hit the heights as the leading all-rounder in the world, and hit the headlines in some less than desirable ways. After a very public departure from Somerset, he had helped Worcestershire into a powerful position at the top of the domestic game and even forced his way back into the England team.

It became clear in the 1991 season that his association with Worcester had run its natural course. He said it would suit him to play out the final chapter of what was by any measure a colourful career in the north of England. There was some talk of Yorkshire relaxing their, until then, strict birth qualification to accommodate him but Durham moved in quickly and his signature sent the county's new interest in the game to fever pitch. A match-winning batsman, intelligent bowler, brilliant fielder and vast personality, Ian Botham was never better than when faced with a challenge. In helping to establish Durham as a first-class county he had that challenge, while Durham and cricket would never be boring with him around.

Several other experienced campaigners were added to the Durham squad. Geoff Cook's old opening partner from Northamptonshire, Wayne Larkins, answered the call. One of the most exciting opening batsmen in the game, he had reached a stage where his career at Northampton was winding down and could be invigorated by new surroundings. Paul Parker was in a similar situation at Sussex. An elegant, effective batsman, he was undoubtedly one of the finest fielders ever seen in the English game. Those two would provide a wealth of experience and, potentially, numerous runs scored quickly enough to be of value to the bowlers.

Phil Bainbridge, another recruit to Durham's cause, had been David Graveney's vice-captain at Gloucestershire for many years. He was also a highly competitive all-rounder who had come close to winning international honours. So, too, had Simon Hughes when a more-than-promising fast bowler with Middlesex. That county had employed a long list of overseas quick bowlers and, consequently, Hughes' chances were more limited than was good for someone who needed constant reassurance to realise his full potential. He had been contemplating a full-time career in journalism when the lure of returning to his old student haunts in Durham kept him in the game.

Of the remaining players with first-class experience to sign for Durham, Phil Berry had had limited opportunities with his native Yorkshire as an off-break bowler, while Ian

Smith, a Durham man, had not fulfilled his potential as an all-rounder with Glamorgan. Steve McEwan had been capped as a quick bowler by Worcestershire in 1989, yet by 1991 did not feature in their plans. Wicket-keeper Chris Scott had also been capped, by Nottinghamshire, but had not been able to command a first-team place unless Bruce French was injured or on international duty. Gary Brown had played a few matches for Middlesex as an opening batsman before joining Durham as early as 1988 and establishing himself in the side. His namesake, Simon Brown, was a promising left-arm fast-medium bowler, with experience at Northamptonshire, now returned to his native county of Durham.

The remaining players in the squad included some who had played county second-eleven cricket and were looking for a first-team opportunity. Darren Blenkiron and Mark Briers fell into this category. Both had joined Durham for the 1991 season and had made enough of an impression to be offered contracts; another 1991 debutant, John Wood, a tall quick bowler from Bradford League cricket, was also offered terms.

Andrew Fothergill had played as a wicket-keeper for Durham since 1982 and made the transition to the first-class staff, while John Glendenen, who made such an impact in 1991, had been a Durham player since 1988. James Daley was a young Durham batsman who had been honing his promising skills on the Lord's ground staff, as had Gary Wigham, a lofty pace bowler from Bishop Auckland. Paul Henderson was only sixteen when he made his Durham debut as a sharpish medium-pace bowler in 1991. That was also when Stewart Hutton appeared on the scene. A left-hand batsman, he headed the county's averages in 1991.

The Durham County Cricket Club Yearbook for 1992

listed the playing staff, with their achievements, backgrounds and playing records (correct as at 1 November 1991) as follows:

Philip Bainbridge

Educated at Hanley High School, Stoke on Trent Sixth Form College and Borough Road College of Education. Born at Sneyd Green, Stoke-on-Trent, Staffordshire, on 16 April 1958.

A right-hand bat and right-arm medium-pace bowler. Made first-class debut for Gloucestershire in 1977, playing for the county between 1977 and 1990, and being awarded his cap in 1981 and a benefit in 1989. One of *Wisden*'s Five Cricketers of the Year in 1985. Scored a thousand runs in a season eight times, his best season being 1985, when he scored 1,644 runs. His highest individual score in first-class cricket, 169, was made against Yorkshire at Cheltenham in 1988, and his best bowling figures, 8 for 53, came against Somerset at Bristol in 1986. He has won one NatWest and two Benson & Hedges individual awards. In the NatWest Trophy his highest score is 89, made against Leicestershire at Leicester in 1989, and his best bowling 3 for 49 against Scotland at Bristol in 1983. In the Benson & Hedges Cup his highest score is 96 against Hampshire at Southampton in 1988, with his best bowling figures being 3 for 21 against Nottinghamshire at Gloucester in 1981. 106 not out against Somerset at Bristol in 1986 is his highest score in the Sunday League, while his best bowling was 5 for 22 against Middlesex at Lord's in 1987. He made his debut for Durham in the Minor Counties Championship in 1991, with a top score of 69 not out against Lincolnshire at Lincoln, and best bowling figures of 3 for 22 against Bedfordshire at Luton. He played as a professional for Leyland Cricket Club in 1991.

Philip John Berry

Educated at Saltscar Comprehensive School and Longlands College of Further Education in Redcar. Born at Saltburn, Yorkshire, on 28 December 1966.

A right-hand batsman and off-break bowler. He made his first-class debut for Yorkshire in 1986. His highest score in first-class cricket, 31 not out, was made in 1990 against Northamptonshire at Headingley, and his best bowling, 2 for 35, was recorded against Cambridge University at Fenner's. His best bowling figures in the County Championship are 1 for 10. For Yorkshire II his best performances were 119 against Northamptonshire at York, and 6 for 77 against Middlesex at Harrow in 1990. He played for Saltburn, Middlesbrough, and Yeadon in the Bradford League.

Darren Andrew Blenkiron

Educated at Bishop Barrington Comprehensive School, Bishop Auckland. Born at Solihull, Warwickshire, on 4 February 1974.

A left-hand batsman and right-arm medium-pace bowler. He made his Durham debut in 1991, with a highest score of 71 against Hertfordshire at Hartlepool and a best bowling performance of 2 for 7 against Durham University at the Racecourse ground. He is the son of Bill Blenkiron, who played for Warwickshire between 1964 and 1974. Darren represented England in Canada in the 1991 International Youth Tournament and went on the England Under-19 tour to Pakistan in 1992. He was just 16 years of age when he made his debut for Gloucestershire II, and scored 136 against Kent II at Canterbury. He plays for Bishop Auckland in the North Yorkshire and South Durham League, but has yet to appear in first class cricket.

Ian Terrence Botham

Educated at Buckler's Mead Secondary School, Yeovil. Born at Heswall, Cheshire, on 24 November 1955.

A right-hand batsman and right-arm medium-pace bowler, he made his debut for Somerset in 1974, playing for that county until 1986. He was awarded his county cap in 1976, was captain in 1984 and 1985, and received a benefit in 1984. He was one of *Wisden*'s Five Cricketers of the Year in 1977. He was formerly on the MCC ground staff at Lord's. As at 1 November 1991 he had played in 99 Tests and been captain in 12, and 99 one-day internationals. His highest score in Tests is 208 against India at the Oval in 1982, while his best bowling figures are 8 for 34 against Pakistan at Lord's in 1978. He made his debut for Worcestershire in 1987, when he was awarded his cap, and played there until the end of the 1991 season. He played for Queensland in the 1987–88 Australian season. He has scored 1,000 runs in a season four times, with 1,530 in 1985 his best performance. That season he hit a record 80 6s in first-class cricket. His highest score is 228 for Somerset against Gloucestershire at Taunton in 1980, while his best bowling in the County Championship is 7 for 54 for Worcestershire against Warwickshire at Worcester in 1991. In 1978 he took 100 wickets in the season, including a hat-trick while playing for MCC. He has won 4 man-of-the-match awards in the NatWest Trophy and 9 in the Benson & Hedges Cup. In the NatWest his best performances are 101 for Worcestershire against Devon at Worcester in 1987, and 5 for 51 for Worcestershire against Lancashire in 1989. In the Benson & Hedges he has a top score of 138 not out for Worcestershire against Gloucestershire at Bristol in 1990, and best bowling of 5 for 41 for Worcestershire against Yorkshire at Worcester in 1988. His best Sunday League performances are 175 not out for Somerset against

Northamptonshire at Wellingborough in 1986, and 5 for 27 for Worcestershire against Gloucestershire at Gloucester in 1987.

Mark Paul Briers
Educated at Hind Leys College, Shepshed. Born at Kegworth in Leicestershire on 21 April 1968.

A right-hand batsman and leg-break and googly bowler. He played for Leicestershire II between 1986 and 1990, was on the staff at Worcestershire playing second-eleven cricket in 1988 and 1989, and appeared for Northamptonshire II in 1990. His best performances in second-eleven cricket were 134 not out for Worcestershire II against Northamptonshire II at Bedford School in 1989, and 5 for 49, also for Worcestershire II against Northamptonshire II, at Oundle in 1988. He played Minor Counties cricket for Bedfordshire in 1990, scoring 124 against Lincolnshire and taking 6 for 45 against Cumberland. He made his debut for Durham in 1991, with a top score of 90 and best bowling figures of 5 for 71, both coming in the match against Northumberland at Gateshead Fell. He played in South Africa during the winters of 1990/1 and 1991/2. He played club cricket for Leicester Nomads and as a professional for Thornaby. He has yet to appear in first-class cricket.

Gary Kevin Brown
Educated at Chance Secondary School, Enfield. Born at Welling in Kent on 16 June 1965.

A right-hand batsman and off-break bowler who made his debut in first-class cricket for Middlesex in 1986 against Nottinghamshire at Trent Bridge. He first appeared for Middlesex II in 1983, and had best performances of 103 against Essex II at Harefield in 1986, and 4 for 62, also against Essex II, at Eton Manor in 1983. He is the younger brother of Keith R. Brown of Middlesex. He first appeared for Durham in 1988 and was awarded his county cap in 1990. He has twice reached his highest score of 114, against Suffolk in 1988 and again, not out, against Hertfordshire at Hartlepool in 1991. He scored 103 not out and 89 when representing the Minor Counties against India at Trowbridge in 1990, a match which was designated as first-class. He played his club cricket for Edmonton, Burnmoor, and Sunderland as a professional.

Simon John Emerson Brown

Educated at Boldon Comprehensive School, Boldon. Born at Cleadon, County Durham, on 29 June 1969.

A right-hand batsman and left-arm fast-medium bowler who made his first-class debut for Northamptonshire against Cambridge University at Fenner's in 1987. That was a year after his debut for Northamptonshire II, for whom his highest score was 52 against Nottinghamshire II at Trent Bridge in 1988. His best bowling figures of 6 for 60 were also recorded for Northamptonshire II against Nottinghamshire II, at Shireoaks in 1990. He went on the England Young Cricketers tour of Sri Lanka in 1986/7. His best performances in first-class cricket for Northamptonshire were 25 not out against Gloucestershire at Northampton in 1988, and 3 for 20 against Oxford University in The Parks, also in 1988. His best bowling in the County Championship was 2 for 11 against Glamorgan at Swansea in 1987. His best bowling performance in the Sunday League was 3 for 26 against Leicestershire at Leicester in 1990. He made his debut for Durham in 1991, with a highest score of 10 not out against Surrey in the Tilcon Trophy at Harrogate. His best bowling figures of 5 for 60 came against Norfolk at Durham University. He played club cricket as a professional with South Shields.

James Arthur Daley

Educated at Hetton Comprehensive School. Born in Sunderland, County Durham, on 24 September 1973.

A right-hand batsman who made his debut for Durham in 1991, scoring 15 not out and 26 on his only appearance. He spent 1991 with the MCC Young Cricketers at Lord's, hitting three centuries. He played his club cricket with Eppleton in the Durham Senior League, but has yet to appear in first-class cricket.

Andrew Robert Fothergill

Educated at Eastbourne Comprehensive School in Darlington. Born in Newcastle upon Tyne on 10 February 1962.

A right-hand batsman and wicket-keeper, he made his first-class debut for the Minor Counties representative side against the Indians at Trowbridge in 1990. His first match for Durham was in 1982, with his highest score for the county, 61, being recorded against Staffordshire at Brewood in 1991. He holds the Durham record for the most stumpings in a match, 5, against Bedfordshire at Luton in 1989 and, with 140 victims, is third in the list of career dismissals. As well as the match against India in 1990, he has also represented the Minor Counties against the West Indies in 1991 and in the Benson & Hedges Cup. He appeared for Derbyshire II in 1985, and played his club cricket with Darlington. He was nominated as the Newcastle Building Society 'Durham Player of the Year' in 1991. He also played soccer for Crook Town, Bishop Auckland and Spennymoor United.

John David Glendenen

Educated at Ormesby Secondary School, Middlesbrough. Born in Middlesbrough on 20 June 1965.

A right-hand batsman who first appeared for Durham in

1988 and was awarded his county cap in 1990. His highest score for the county is 200 not out, scored in the Britannic Invitation match against Victoria at Durham University in 1991, when he became only the second player to pass 200 in Durham's 109-year history, after E.W. Elliott's 217 not out in 1906 and 201 in 1903. His highest score in the Minor Counties Championship was 130 against Northumberland at Jesmond in 1990. Between 1983 and 1986 he appeared with Yorkshire II, and for Gloucestershire II in 1988 and Somerset II in 1989. He scored 109 against Glamorgan at Darlington in the 1991 NatWest Trophy match. His club cricket was played for Middlesbrough, Marske, and Easington Colliery Welfare as a professional. He played in Australia in the winters of 1990/1 and 1991/2. He has yet to appear in first-class cricket.

David Anthony Graveney

Educated at Millfield School. Born in Bristol on 2 January 1953, the son of Ken Graveney, who played for Gloucestershire between 1947 and 1964, and nephew of Tom Graveney of Gloucestershire, Worcestershire, Queensland and England.

A right-hand batsman and slow left-arm bowler who made his first-class debut for Gloucestershire in 1972. He played for that county until 1990, being awarded his county cap in 1976, was captain from 1981 until 1988, and was granted a benefit in 1986. He played for Somerset in 1991. He was manager of the England XI tour to South Africa in 1989/90. His highest score of 119 was for Gloucestershire against Oxford University in The Parks in 1980, while his highest score in the County Championship, 105 not out, was recorded the following season against Northamptonshire at Bristol. His best bowling figures were 8 for 85 for Gloucestershire against Nottinghamshire at Cheltenham in

1974. He performed the hat-trick in 1983. The most wickets he took in a single season was 73 in 1976. He won 2 NatWest man-of-the-match awards. His best performances in the 60-overs competitions were 44 for Gloucestershire against Surrey in the Gillette Cup at Bristol in 1973, and 5 for 11 for Gloucestershire against Ireland in Dublin in 1981 in the NatWest Trophy. In the Benson & Hedges Cup he scored 49 not out against Somerset at Taunton in 1982, and took 3 for 13 for Gloucestershire against Nottinghamshire at Bristol in 1985, with his best bowling figures of 4 for 22 being recorded against Hampshire at Lydney in 1974. He was appointed captain of Durham for the 1992 season.

Paul William Henderson

Educated at Billingham Campus School and Bede Sixth Form College. Born at Stockton-on-Tees on 22 October 1974.

A right-hand batsman and right-arm medium-fast bowler. He made his debut for Durham in 1991 at the age of 16. His highest score was 61 not out against Cumberland at Barrow-in-Furness and he recorded best bowling figures of 4 for 22 against Denmark at Norton. His best bowling figures in the Minor Counties Championship were 4 for 32 against Northumberland at Gateshead Fell. He played club cricket for Middlesbrough and will continue with his studies in 1992. He has yet to appear in first-class cricket.

Simon Peter Hughes

Educated at Latymer Upper School in Hammersmith, and Durham University. Born at Kingston upon Thames in Surrey on 20 December 1959.

A right-hand batsman and right-arm fast-medium bowler, he made his first-class debut for Middlesex in 1980, was awarded his county cap in 1981 and remained with Middlesex until the end of the 1991 season, his benefit year. He played for Northern Transvaal in South Africa in the winter of 1982/3. His highest score in first-class cricket was 53 against Cambridge University at Fenner's in 1988, while his highest score in the County Championship was 47 against Warwickshire at Uxbridge in 1986. His best bowling figures, 7 for 35, were recorded against Surrey at the Oval in 1986, the year he took 63 wickets in his best season. He won one NatWest Trophy man-of-the-match award, and his best performances in that competition were both recorded against Durham at Darlington in 1989, when he scored 11 and took 4 for 20. His highest score in the Benson & Hedges Cup was 22 against Somerset at Taunton in 1990, three years after his best bowling figures of 4 for 34 came against the same county at Lord's. In the Sunday League his best performances were 22 not out against Surrey at Lord's in 1985 and 5 for 23 against Worcestershire at Worcester in 1989.

Stewart Hutton
Educated at De Brus School, Skelton. Born at Stockton-on-Tees, County Durham, on 30 November 1969.

A left-hand batsman who made his Durham debut in 1991 and headed the batting averages with 454 runs from 10 innings at an average of 56.75. He scored 4 50s and one century, 112 not out against Norfolk at Durham University. He played his club cricket for Guisborough and represented the North Yorkshire & South Durham League XI in 1991 after scoring prolifically in club cricket. He was named as the 'Sunday Sun North-east Cricketer of the Year' in 1991. He played for Yorkshire II in 1990 but has yet to appear in first-class cricket.

Dean Mervyn Jones
Born at Coburg, Melbourne, Australia, on 24 March 1961.

A right-hand batsman and off-break bowler, he made his first-class debut for Victoria in the 1981/2 season. His highest score was made when touring England with the Australians in 1989, 248 against Warwickshire at Edgbaston. His best bowling figures in first-class cricket are 1 for 0. He had played in 44 Tests for Australia by 1 November 1991, and 115 one-day internationals. His Test debut was in 1984 against the West Indies in Port of Spain. He had hit two double-centuries in Tests, with 216 against the West Indies in Adelaide in 1989 and 210 against India at Madras in 1986, as well as 9 single Test centuries. He had hit 7 centuries in one-day internationals, with 145 his highest score and 2 for 45 his best bowling return. In that highest first-class innings, against Warwickshire in 1989, he hit a record 12 6s on his first-class debut for the Australians in England. He scored 144 against Durham for Victoria in the Britannic Invitation match at Durham University in 1991, and played cricket in the north-east in the Callers-Pegasus Cricket Festival.

Wayne Larkins

Educated at Bushmead Secondary School, Eaton Socon. Born at Roxton in Bedfordshire on 22 November 1953.

A right-hand batsman and right-arm medium-pace bowler who made his first-class debut for Northamptonshire in 1972. He played for that county until 1991, and was awarded his county cap in 1976 and a benefit year in 1986. Between 1982 and 1984 he spent the winters in South Africa playing for Eastern Provinces. He appeared in 10 Tests and 25 one-day internationals. His highest score in Tests was 54 against the West Indies at Port of Spain in 1989/90, and in one-day internationals he has a highest score of 124. In first-class cricket, 252 for Northamptonshire against Glamorgan in Cardiff in 1983 stands as the high mark. A year later he recorded his best bowling figures of 5 for 59 against Worcestershire at Worcester. He has scored 1,000 runs in a season 11 times, with his best season being 1982, when he scored 1,863 runs. He has scored 49 first-class centuries. He has won 2 awards in the NatWest Trophy and 5 in the Benson & Hedges Cup. His best performances in the other one-day competitions are 121 not out against Essex at Chelmsford in 1987 and 2 for 38 against Gloucestershire at Bristol in 1985 in the NatWest Trophy; in the Benson & Hedges Cup he scored 132 against Warwickshire at Edgbaston in 1982 and took 4 for 37 against the Combined Universities at Northampton in 1980; in the Sunday League he scored 172 not out against Warwickshire at Luton in 1983 and took 5 for 32 against Essex at Ilford in 1978.

Steven Michael McEwan

Educated at Worcester Royal Grammar School. Born at Worcester on 5 May 1962.

A right-hand batsman and right-arm fast-medium bowler who played for Worcestershire between 1985 and 1991 and was awarded his county cap in 1989, but who did not appear in the County Championship in 1991. His highest score in first-class cricket was 54 against Yorkshire at Worcester in 1990. His best season with the ball was 1989, when he took 52 wickets, including his best return of 6 for 34 against Leicestershire at Kidderminster. In other competitions his best performances were 6 with the bat and 3 for 51 against Warwickshire at Edgbaston in 1989 in the NatWest Trophy, and 2 for 53 in the Benson & Hedges Cup against Nottinghamshire at Trent Bridge in 1990. In the Sunday League he scored 18 not out against Yorkshire at Worcester in 1990 and took 4 for 35 against Derbyshire, again at Worcester in 1990.

Paul William Giles Parker

Educated at Collyer's Grammar School and St Catharine's College, Cambridge University. Born in Bulawayo, Rhodesia, on 15 January 1956.

A right-hand batsman and right-arm medium-pace bowler who first appeared in first-class cricket in 1976, when he made his debuts for Cambridge University and Sussex. He won Blues at Cambridge in 1976, 1977 and 1978, and played for Sussex between 1976 and 1991. He was awarded his county cap in 1979 and captained the county between 1988 and 1991. He appeared in one Test, against Australia at the Oval in 1981, where his top score was 13. His most successful season was 1984, when he scored 1,692 runs, one of 8 times he has scored 1,000 runs in a season, and he has hit 41 centuries. His highest score in first-class cricket is 215 for Cambridge University against Essex at Fenner's in 1976. He scored 181 for Sussex against Sri Lanka at Hove in 1981, while in the County Championship his best was 140 against Gloucestershire at Hove in 1984. His best first-class bowling figures were recorded at Guildford against Surrey in 1984, 2 for 21. He has won 4 man-of-the-match awards in the NatWest Trophy and 5 in the Benson & Hedges Cup. His best performances in the NatWest are 109 against Ireland at Hove in 1985 and 1 for 10. In the Benson & Hedges they are 87 against Leicestershire at Hove in 1991 and 2 for 3 against the Minor Counties at Hove in 1987. In the Sunday League he scored 121 not out against Northamptonshire at Hastings in 1983 and has taken 1 for 2.

Christopher Wilmot Scott

Educated at Robert Pattinson Comprehensive School. Born at Thorpe on the Hill in Lincolnshire on 23 January 1964.

A right-hand batsman and wicket-keeper, he made his first-class debut for Nottinghamshire in 1981, playing for that county until 1991 and being awarded his county cap in 1988. His highest score in first-class cricket is 78 against Cambridge University at Fenner's in 1983, and in the County Championship 69 not out against Warwickshire at Trent Bridge in 1986. He held a record 10 catches in a match for Nottinghamshire against Derbyshire at Derby in 1988. His highest score in the Benson & Hedges Cup is 18 against Northamptonshire at Northampton in 1988, and in the Sunday League 26 against Yorkshire at Trent Bridge in 1987. His highest score in second-eleven cricket is 96 for Nottinghamshire II against Derbyshire II at Heanor in 1990. He made his Durham debut in the Britannic Invitation match against Victoria at Durham University in 1991.

Ian Smith

Educated at Ryton Comprehensive School. Born at Chopwell, County Durham, on 11 March 1967.

A right-hand batsman and right-arm medium-pace bowler who made his first-class debut for Glamorgan in 1985 and played for them until 1991. His highest score was 116 against Kent at Canterbury in 1989, with best bowling figures of 3 for 48 against Hampshire in Cardiff in the same season. His best performances in the NatWest Trophy were 33 against Hampshire in Cardiff in 1989 and 3 for 60 against Durham at Darlington in 1991. In the Benson & Hedges Cup he scored 21 against Worcestershire at Worcester in 1990, and took 1 for 21. In the Sunday League 56 not out against Warwickshire at Aberystwyth was his best, along with 3 for 22 against Hampshire at Cardiff in 1989. He represented Durham Under-15s at cricket and had trials with several Football League clubs.

Gary Wigham
Educated at Bishop Barrington Comprehensive School, Bishop Auckland. Born at Bishop Auckland, County Durham, on 2 March 1973.

A right-hand batsman and six-foot-six-inch-tall right-arm fast-medium bowler. Appeared once for Durham, against Hertfordshire at Hartlepool in 1991. During 1991 he was with the MCC Young Cricketers at Lord's, and in 1990 had appeared twice for Northamptonshire II, scoring 42 against Lancashire II at Northampton. He attended the same school as Darren Blenkiron, played his club cricket for Bishop Auckland, and played in New Zealand in 1991/2. He has yet to appear in first-class cricket.

John Wood
Educated at Crofton High School and Leeds Polytechnic. Born in Wakefield on 22 July 1970.

A six-foot-three-inch-tall batsman and right-arm fast-medium bowler. He made his debut for Durham in 1991, scoring 40 not out against Cambridgeshire at Fenner's and taking 5 for 22 against Bedfordshire at Luton, with 8 for 36 in the match. His club cricket was played with Spen Victoria in the Bradford League. He has yet to play first-class cricket.

When Geoff Cook had completed his playing staff for 1992 there was a good deal of criticism, albeit mainly from outside the borders of Durham. 'A collection of ageing mercenaries in search of one-day respectability' was one unflattering description of the Durham squad. Yet the facts do not bear out that criticism. Of the twenty-two players on the staff, thirteen had a definite connection with the north-east before they were recruited for 1992. The average age as at 1 January 1992 was only twenty-six years and six months, even with four players of thirty-five or over.

In all team sports it is as well to have the oft-cited blend of youthful enthusiasm and battle-hardened experience. The young players can instil their more senior brethren with some, perhaps forgotten, exuberance, while the older players can use their experience to protect and instruct the youngsters. The senior players all had new responsibilities in the Durham structure. David Graveney and Paul Parker had been county captains, and Ian Botham had captained England. Men like Simon Hughes and Wayne Larkins had more responsibility than they might have had before, but shouldering it should bring out the best in their own games and those of the young bowlers and batsmen.

As far as ambition was concerned, there was no doubt that a one-day competition offered Durham the best chance of making an immediate impact. There was a general feeling that a solid mid-table finish in the County Championship would be more than respectable, especially if Durham played their matches in an attractive fashion. There was no doubting that a varied attack should be able to perform in most conditions, yet there remained a nagging doubt as to whether that attack would have sufficient penetration to lift Durham up among the title contenders in their early days as a first-class county.

The batsmen could score runs quickly, but there was little prospect early in Durham's first-class career of their being set chaseable totals by generous declarations; no county would want to be the first to suffer defeat at the hands of the new boys. Those same batsmen, however, would be able to exploit situations in which counties in contention for the title needed to offer the carrot to give themselves the chance of a win. Similarly, if the batsmen could score enough runs as quickly as appeared likely, the chances of winning three- or four-day matches would become that much greater.

In the limited-overs competitions – where the require-ment has always been for the containing, rather than attacking, bowling, and for fast, heavy run-scoring – the attack appeared more than adequate to the task, while one-day cricket could have been invented to show off the batting line-up at its best. It would be important to have a good showing in at least one competition to keep up the momentum of the first-class launch. Having expended so much energy in getting everything else just right, it was unlikely that Durham would fall down on bringing together a playing staff that would measure up to the challenge ahead.

8

The Realisation of a Dream

In the months leading up to the outbreak of the First World War, German naval officers ended formal dinners with a special toast to 'Der Tag' or 'the day'. The day in question was that on which they would go into action against the Royal Navy. As the moment of reckoning came ever closer for Durham, so the expectation, anticipation, and not a little apprehension, grew. Many a silent toast was drunk in County Durham as they moved towards their 'day', Tuesday 14 April 1992, when a Durham side would take the field at Oxford for the very first time as a first-class county.

On the business side, it was Durham County Cricket Club Limited that was anticipating the great day so keenly. When the officers and members went into the 1991 annual general meeting in March, they did so as a committee; they emerged as the board of directors of a new company limited by guarantee. This was a revolutionary step in cricket. In other sports there were clubs that were limited companies, but Durham was the first first-class county cricket club to be thus constituted.

The enterprising step had been taken with the full encouragement of the TCCB. It was well known that the committee system had its drawbacks. It was often difficult to promote change, especially if there was the merest hint of contention about a proposal. Many clubs had antiquated constitutions and far too many members on their general committees to allow the necessary majority to be obtained when it came to a vote.

Durham's new structure for a new club would be watched very closely by everyone else. The county was being used as a testing ground. If other counties saw the idea of a limited company working efficiently and successfully, some might well follow the same path. The early evidence was that the system was working in Durham. The directors confined themselves to running a million-pound business and did not get involved in the cricket side unless, of course, there were business decisions to be made regarding contracts or the like.

At that 1991 annual general meeting, Arthur Austin stood down as chairman. He had held the position since 1975 but felt the time had come for a change, in view of the club's changing circumstances. He was installed as its United Kingdom patron. As an indication of the esteem this appointment reflected, the overseas patron was none other than Sir Donald Bradman.

Don Robson was elected chairman of the board. Also appointed to the board was the former treasurer Tom Moffat. Four other directors were elected: Matt Roseberry, Bob Jackson of the Durham Cricket Association, an accountant by the name of Bill Milner, and Neil Riddell, the former captain of the county club. All had been on the county committee before, all were cricket-orientated, and between them could bring to bear a range of business experience and expertise. They, in turn, co-opted three more members to the board, namely Roy Caller, Joe Sherrington, and a solicitor, Ian Mills. Others could be recruited to fulfil special functions as required.

A radical organisation was in place for the 1992 season

and Durham's entry into first-class cricket. Before that, there was a last summer of competition in the Minor Counties Championship. Having been joint winners the first time they had played in it, back in 1895, there would have been an appealing symmetry had Durham won the last championship in which they appeared. There were, however, more important issues to be decided than the mere winning of another title.

Geoff Cook wanted to use the final season of Minor Counties cricket to have a good look at some players to whom contracts might be offered. He wanted to see how they would react under pressure and whether they were likely to measure up to the high standards he expected. He took over the captaincy of the side himself, and when the required situations did not materialise in the course of a game, he manufactured them. For instance, when a wicket looked as if it might have 200 runs in it for the final innings, he might declare 180 runs in front, to put extra pressure on his bowlers.

Those who wilted in the face of that pressure, or even refused the challenge entirely, were not for Durham. Those who strove that little bit harder, and produced the required level of performance in difficult circumstances, came through. It not only proved an excellent means of testing players' mettle, but provided some most entertaining cricket.

Even if a player was found to be wanting, and a contract was not in the offing, he might be considered for the second eleven in 1992, which was going to be captained by Geoff Cook himself. There was no doubt he could still have held down a place in the first team, but that was not part of his brief at Durham. He was there to develop cricket, not for a single season but over a longer period. Some thought he might be tempted to fill the occasional crisis-created vacancy in the first team himself, but he was adamant that he would not do so. If such a situation arose, it would be better to give a young player a chance. Nothing would be proved for the long-term good of Durham if Cook went into the first team and scored a solid 30; whereas the county might benefit immeasurably in the future from the experience and confidence an eighteen-year-old could gain from a similar opportunity. Some players took the opportunities offered them in 1991, others failed; but all had a chance to impress.

The Minor Counties season began with a championship match against the 1990 champions, Hertfordshire, at Hartlepool in May. It was the first time Durham had taken the field since the confirmation of first-class status, and an understandable air of expectancy surrounded the proceedings. Darren Blenkiron and Mark Briers did not waste their first opportunity to impress, scoring 71 and 61, respectively. Durham declared at 188 for 6, and Hertfordshire had lost only 4 wickets when they, in turn, declared, with a first innings lead of 13. Gary Brown was 114 not out and Mark Briers 66 not out when Durham declared at 280 for 3 in their second innings. On what was clearly a rather good batting wicket, Hertfordshire were left 268 to win, and got home by 4 wickets. It was a blow to Durham's championship aspirations, especially as Hertfordshire were also fancied contenders for the title. As it turned out, Hertfordshire did not win another match during the entire season, and even failed to qualify for the NatWest Trophy in 1992. For Durham, some very positive points came out of the exercise, if only two championship ones.

At the start of June, attention turned to the Holt Cup, the Minor Counties knock-out competition. The draw for the first round had paired Durham with Northumberland, the match to be played at Gateshead Fell Cricket Club.

It should have been a festive occasion, but the weather intervened and the match was abandoned without a ball being bowled. The rules of the competition did not allow for the tie to be played on another day, so the teams had to resort to the dreaded bowling competition to decide the outcome – a slightly better method than tossing a coin and at least with the merit of being based on a cricketing skill. This particular contest was won by Northumberland.

It was a full month later that Durham played their next championship match. They had just emerged with some credit from a NatWest first-round tie with Glamorgan at Darlington, but could not register their first win of the season at Brewood against Staffordshire. After John Glendenen had registered a half-century, Durham declared at 182 for 2. Staffordshire declared 9 runs behind with 5 wickets down, before Durham extended their lead to 217 in the second innings. Andrew Fothergill scored 61 of those runs and the captain was 46 not out at the closure. Staffordshire, with their opening pair of Dean and Cartledge in prolific form, reached the target with 5 wickets down.

In mid-July, Durham recorded that first elusive win of the season. The venue was Wardown Park, Luton & Bedfordshire the opponents. Paul Burn, who was in fine form, scored two 50s in the match, John Glendenen notched up 40, and with John Wood returning 5 for 22 in the first innings and 3 for 14 in the second, Durham won by 67 runs, bowling out Bedfordshire for 149 in their second-innings run-chase. It was a conclusive victory, which netted 20 points and gave a timely lift to morale.

After two days in Bedfordshire, the side moved on to Fenner's to meet Cambridgeshire. Several batsmen were running into form, and Mark Briers, Phil Bainbridge, Paul Burn and Gary Brown scored half-centuries. Cambridgeshire started the last innings requiring 267 to win. They had reached 179 for 8 at the close. The sides took two points each from what was certainly a moral victory for Durham.

Another finely balanced game followed at the end of July. Cumberland were the opponents at Barrow-in-Furness. Durham reached 177 for 6 declared, with an encouraging innings of 61 not out from sixteen-year-old Paul Henderson, and a half-century from Mark Briers. Cumberland were also 6 wickets down when they declared 44 runs ahead on the first innings. It is not common in Minor Counties Championship cricket that a side can score in excess of 300 in the third innings of a match and still have a chance of winning, but Durham did just that. Gary Brown scored 90, Mark Briers 78 and Geoff Cook 67 not out, as they reached 308 for 5 declared. Cumberland were 142 for 8, still 123 runs from victory, at the end of an absorbing match.

Durham returned to Gateshead Fell in August for a last Minor Counties Championship match against their oldest opponents, Northumberland. Young Paul Henderson continued to impress, taking 4 for 34, as Northumberland were bowled out for 159. Durham replied with 338 for 9 declared, Mark Briers hitting 90, Stewart Hutton 52, Darren Blenkiron 46 and Geoff Cook 45. Mark Briers took 5 for 71 with his leg-breaks in Northumberland's second innings of 201, and Durham scored the 23 needed to win in their second innings without losing a wicket.

The next game, against Lincolnshire at Lincoln, produced another victory, this time by 5 wickets. Durham declared their first innings closed when still 28 runs behind. Lincolnshire were bowled out for 199 in their second innings. Gary Brown took 4 for 36 and then hit 65 as, with Phil Bainbridge 68 not out, the win was secured.

Gary Brown scored heavily again in the next match, against Norfolk at Durham University's Racecourse Ground.

His 81 and Stewart Hutton's 46 allowed Geoff Cook to declare at 226 for 5. Norfolk got within 35 runs of that total before declaring and Durham appeared to be within sight of a third consecutive victory. A second innings of 250 for 3 declared, with Stewart Hutton scoring an undefeated 112 and John Glendenen 80, set Norfolk 287 to win. It was asking a lot, but there was nothing in the splendid wicket to fear, and the East Anglian side squeezed home with just one wicket in hand, despite Simon Brown's figures of 5 for 60.

Suffolk were the next visitors to County Durham, and it was another last-over finish, which this time went in Durham's favour. John Glendenen hit 85 and Stewart Hutton 54, as Durham made 227 for 5 declared. Suffolk scored 151 all out and Durham increased their lead with 222 for 7 declared in the second innings. As was only fitting in his last game as captain, Geoff Cook was top scorer with 63, and there was yet another promising innings of 42 from John Glendenen. Suffolk were bowled out for 250 in the last over of the match.

It was another example of the exciting cricket played by the team, which had been transformed since the beginning of the season. By its end, they were moving into top gear and were a match for anyone in Minor Counties cricket. Durham finished third in the Eastern Division of the Minor Counties Championship with 103 points. Cumberland were two points and one place higher in a division won by Staffordshire with 114 points. Durham's total would have been enough to win them the Western Division title, and with a little luck they could have won the Eastern Division. Such comments were not made by Durham themselves; they had enjoyed a fine season of cricket that was never boring, and many individuals had made significant progress.

Paul Burn, although not one of the twenty-two registered

on the first-class staff, topped the batting averages. He scored 357 runs in 8 innings to average 59.50, with a top score of 71, displaying an admirable consistency. Mark Briers, Geoff Cook and Gary Brown could all boast averages in excess of forty-five. Andrew Fothergill could claim all-rounder status as a wicket-keeper batsman, with an average of 35. Darren Blenkiron and John Glendenen finished just below the thirty mark, and Glendenen still had his magnificent innings against Victoria to come. Mark Briers headed the bowling averages with 20 wickets at 25.50 each, and Simon Brown also took 20 wickets, at 28.70.

The matches against Victoria proved a highly satisfactory conclusion to Durham's final domestic season as a minor county. The preparations for 1992 did not, however, end in September 1991. There was the opportunity for the players to get together at the McEwans Indoor Centre. It was noticeable how good senior, experienced players like Paul Parker and Wayne Larkins were in helping the batsmen. Simon Hughes did a similar job with the seam bowlers, and throughout there was an air of excitement at the challenge ahead and an air of togetherness.

This positive mood had the chance to express itself in February, when a party of players went to Zimbabwe. Because of other commitments it was not the full Durham side, but the trip proved of immense value in establishing a sense of identity among the players. Until then, they had been associated with a concept rather than belonging to a reality. Now there was an opportunity for the youngsters to appreciate the standards to which they had to aspire, and for the senior players to set those standards. It was no good relying on a reputation, they had to show that they could play and behave as demanded by their new circumstances.

It was a testing tour in every respect. At some stage

or another during the tour they would meet most of the players who were about to rub shoulders with the very best in the World Cup in Australia. The conditions in which the matches were played would also cause plenty of problems. It was not easy to move from the depths of winter in north-east England to African temperatures that were always over ninety degrees Fahrenheit on match days, and twice, at Mutare and Bulawayo, exceeded double figures.

There was little time for acclimatisation, either. It was effectively a case of going straight from the airport to the Harare South Country Club and playing a 50-overs-a-side match against virtually the full Zimbabwe XI. So, it was not altogether surprising that Zimbabwe won by 123 runs, having made 274 for 4 in their 50 overs. Durham were 151 for 8 at the close of their innings, with only John Glendenen, who scored 41, looking the part. For the record, Wayne Larkins, Paul Parker, Ian Smith (an ironically appropriate name, given the venue!), Phil Berry and David Graveney all made their Durham debuts. For the historians, it could go down as Durham's first match as a first-class county.

The next day, 4 February, the two sides met again at the Alexandra Sports Club in Harare. This time Durham batted first and compiled a respectable 206 for 4 in their 50 overs. John Glendenen again impressed with 49, while Phil Bainbridge scored 64 and Gary Brown weighed in with 39. Zimbabwe had one over and 2 wickets to spare when they recorded their second victory in two days. This time it had been a much closer contest.

After a rest day, there was a match against Zimbabwe Under-19s at the Old Hararians Sports Club in Harare. Gary Wigham impressed with a fine stint of bowling to finish with figures of 9-4-10-3, with each of his victims being bowled. The Zimbabweans were bowled out for

152 in 47.1 overs and Durham cruised to a comfortable 6-wicket victory with four overs in hand. Mark Briers with 63 and Paul Henderson with 36 were undefeated at the end, after a partnership of 105 in ninety-two minutes. They had something to celebrate, as did Paul Parker, captaining the side in the absence of David Graveney, and sixteen-year-old Neil Killeen, making his county debut.

In another 50-overs-a-side match at the Harare South Country Club, Zimbabwe Country Districts were the opponents. A total of 200 for 7 by Durham, having been put in to bat, appeared to be the minimum that was required. James Daley top-scored with 47, and without that contribution it would have been scarcely a defensible total. Even with it, it was a desperately close-run thing. The Country Districts were going well at 163 for 4 when Phil Bainbridge took two wickets in the same over. As Simon Brown bowled the last ball of the match, the home side's total stood at 199 for 6; one run to bring the scores level and two runs to win. With the help of a catch by Mark Briers, Brown took the wicket that ensured a win for Durham by a single run.

A Zimbabwe XI inflicted a 13-run defeat in the next 50-over match at the Harare Sports Club. Despite Gary Brown's half-century, Durham were bowled out for 187 in 48.5 overs. Three run-outs did not help the cause.

It was perhaps not the sort of preparation Durham would have chosen for the first three-day match of their programme, but several hurdles were being overcome as the side began to organise itself into an identifiable unit. The tour was proving its worth even if not all the results were going Durham's way.

The opponents at the Mutare Sports Club on 11, 12 and 13 February were a Manicaland Select XI. Gary Wigham and David Graveney took four wickets each as the home side were bowled out for 220. Scores in excess of fifty from

Phil Bainbridge, Ian Smith and Mark Briers allowed David
Graveney to declare at 300 for 7 and have another bowl at
Manicaland before the close of the second day. The Durham
attack, however, failed to make the same inroads into the
batting as before. The Manicaland batsman Nigel Hough
scored 200 not out from only 261 deliveries, and the home
side declared at 286 for 2.

To win, Durham needed to score 207 at a brisk rate.
They had a maximum of seventy minutes plus 20 overs.
Wayne Larkins set about the task in dramatic fashion.
He played an innings of controlled aggression, gradually
lifting the tempo as he began to dominate the attack. He
scored 119 from only 114 balls, including 4 6s and 14 4s.
The scoring rate indicates how well he controlled the pace
of the innings. Durham's first fifty came in even time off
13 overs. The hundred came up in the twenty-first over,
thirty minutes later. Twenty-seven minutes were needed for
the next fifty, which was posted in the twenty-eighth over,
while two hundred was reached for the loss of 2 wickets in
131 minutes in the thirty-fifth over. Larkins and Ian Smith,
who scored 55 not out, put on 160 for the third wicket in just
eighty-five minutes.

Larkins was out with just one more boundary needed
to reach the target. That was attained without further
loss and with nine balls of the match remaining. It was
Wayne Larkins' maiden century for Durham, scored in his
best style. Geoff Cook, who had seen him devour attacks
in this way when they opened the batting together for
Northamptonshire, now had reassurance that the runs and
ability were still there. If Wayne Larkins could reproduce
that form in the English season to come, Durham would be
able to chase any target with confidence.

It was back to the Harare Sports Club for what turned
out to be perhaps the most disappointing game of the

tour. After being bowled out for 120 in 45 overs of a 50-overs-a-side match by the President's XI, there was no way back for Durham. The President's XI won by 9 wickets. The result did not augur well for the next match – the historic meeting with another visiting side from England, Buckinghamshire.

Although Durham and Buckinghamshire shared the record of nine Minor Counties Championship titles, the two sides had never met until the 50-overs-a-side match at Alexandra Sports Club, Harare, on Monday 17 February 1992. The traditional challenge match between the winners of the Eastern and Western divisions of the Minor Counties Championship is played over 55 overs, usually, nowadays, in the delightful surroundings of Wardown Park, Luton. The Harare game was to be shorter and the surroundings, though just as delightful, rather more exotic. However, it was still a sort of challenge match between the two counties that, over nearly a century of competition, had proved themselves the leaders of Minor Counties cricket.

Buckinghamshire won the toss and put Durham in to bat. Mark Briers contributed 33 runs, Stewart Hutton 40, and Paul Parker, the acting captain, held the innings together with 63. Even so, a rate of 3.72 runs an over took the score to only 186 for 6 when the innings was closed. Durham's attack in this game was not exactly top-heavy with experience. Eighteen-year-old Gary Wigham shared the new ball with sixteen-year-old Neil Killeen. Ian Smith, all of twenty-four, was first change, followed by seventeen-year-old Paul Henderson. The other bowler used was a real old stager: Phil Berry was twenty-five! For all their youth, they bowled magnificently. Wigham's 10 overs cost 10 runs; Killeen took 2 for 14 in his allotted overs, Smith 1 for 18, Berry 2 for 24, and only Henderson, with 1 for 44, did not have outstanding figures. Keen fielding backed up the fine bowling and Buckinghamshire were restricted to 116 for 7, leaving Durham the winners by 70 runs in a fitting farewell to Minor Counties cricket.

A four-day match against Zimbabwe B was next on the agenda at the Harare Sports Club. Durham had built up a telling momentum and their self-belief was growing all the time. Certainly, Paul Henderson's confidence was given a timely boost. Zimbabwe, batting first, had reached 48 for 1 when Henderson took a hat-trick. He finished with 5 for 51, Simon Brown took 4 for 45 and Zimbabwe were 230 all out. When you bowl a side out just after tea on the first day of a four-day game, it needs only steady batting to build up a big lead, which Durham accordingly provided.

They took their time, but John Glendenen scored 51 and his opening partner Stewart Hutton a studied 143. Gary Brown scored 65 and put on 170 for the second wicket with Hutton, while Paul Parker was exactly 100 not out at the declaration, which came after he and Phil Berry had shared a century partnership for the seventh wicket. Berry was 51 not out and Durham's total was 447 for 6. Berry the bowler then did his stuff, taking 4 for 47 as Zimbabwe were bowled out for just 127, including a stand of 42 for the last wicket. Durham won by an innings and 90 runs.

There was certainly no shortage of limited-overs cricket on the tour of Zimbabwe. Sunday 23 February saw the team at the Bulawayo Athletic Club ground, giving Paul Parker the chance to play cricket in his place of birth. A Zimbabwe XI found the left-arm spin of David Graveney just a little too testing. He took 3 for 22 in his 10 overs as they were bowled out for 144. Wayne Larkins and John Glendenen opened Durham's reply with a partnership of 112 in even time, Larkins scoring 69 and Glendenen 37, and Durham won by 4 wickets with 14 overs and a ball to spare.

To conclude the tour there was a three-day game against

the same opposition at the same venue. Durham set the pace with 316 for 6 declared in their first innings. Mark Briers scored a fine 132 not out, Wayne Larkins a typically flamboyant 71 from 49 balls, including 4 6s and 7 4s, and Chris Scott a more careful 47. The Zimbabwe XI made 262 in a minute longer than Durham had taken, before declaring with 6 wickets down, and Durham could aim for the important third declaration of the match. Stewart Hutton's 54 and Mark Briers' 30, before he retired hurt, set the scene for Phil Bainbridge and Wayne Larkins. In an unbroken partnership they put on 43 in a quarter of an hour, and Durham declared at 202 for 4 after lunch. Phil Berry with 4 wickets and David Graveney with 3 very nearly spun Durham to victory. Set 257 to win in 130 minutes plus 20 overs, the Zimbabwe XI were 205 for 9 at the close, after their last pair had survived for twelve minutes without scoring a run.

Durham learnt much in Africa. Just as they had in the last season of Minor Counties cricket, they got better and better as they went along. Results and performances improved, and the team settled down as an effective, efficient unit. The opposition was not always of first-class standard, and they were not likely to experience temperatures in the nineties or more at the Racecourse Ground in April. However, Durham had done more than enough to suggest that they were making serious progress towards becoming a competitive unit. And there was more to come: Ian Botham, Dean Jones, Simon Hughes and Steve McEwan would all add immeasurably to the quality of the side.

Ian Botham, in particular, was already making a contribution to the Durham cause through his performances for England in the World Cup. There was a noticeable jump in the number of membership applications every time he did something of note in Australia and New Zealand. When he won the man-of-the-match award for his performance against Australia in Sydney, it was announced from Durham that membership had reached very nearly 4,000 and was rising all the time. It was a signal from the public that he and the rest of the team had been accepted.

So the countdown to the season was on. Geoff Cook admitted that the enormity of what was about to happen had begun to dawn on him, but it was nothing more than a healthy pumping of adrenalin prior to the big day. Because others were likely to feel that pressure too, he deliberately designed a truncated programme of pre-season activities. There would be no prolonged build-up of nets, fitness training, and a long list of friendlies. Just two one-day friendly matches were arranged: against the County Champions, Essex, at Chelmsford on 11 and 12 April. Then, Oxford University awaited on Tuesday 14 April. In a way, that big day would be made slightly anti-climactic by the fact that a friendly match was to usher in the first-class era of Durham County Cricket Club. However, it was useful from a cricketing point of view that here was another gentle step in the transition from minor to major. From a historical viewpoint, everyone was looking ahead to the first County Championship match.

The north-east of England was noted for its proud tradition of shipbuilding. The SS Durham County Cricket Club had been planned with a care and attention to detail reminiscent of the shipbuilding industry. The design was at the same time breathtaking and practical. The engines had power and efficiency and were already tested to run smoothly. The construction was sturdy. The good ship just needed a last lick of paint here and there, and then it would glide down the slipway into the water, giving a confident blast on the siren before moving out to the open sea. God bless all who sail in her.

Appendix: The First Fixtures

Oxford University v. Durham (Friendly)

On Tuesday 14 April at eleven o'clock, an Oxford under-graduate by the name of Michael Jeh ran in to bowl to John Glendenen, and Durham's first-class adventure had begun. It was a typical April day in The Parks, with grey skies and a cold wind laced with drizzle. By lunchtime that drizzle had developed into steady rain, and the rest of Durham's first day in first-class cricket was washed out. The second day was lost completely, and it was not until the third day that Glendenen and Paul Parker could resume their partnership.

When the first day was brought to a premature close, the Durham openers had reached 119 from the 34 overs bowled, having been put in to bat by the University. Glendenen had reached 64 and Parker 50 against an attack that was never likely to rip through the batting order but which demanded a certain respect. In all respects it was a satisfactory opening for Durham in that there were runs on the board and the first of the emotional hurdles had been cleared with ease. There had been rather more interest than usual in the University's first day of cricket, with some two hundred spectators and an array of cameras, commentators and scribes to witness the historic moment.

When play resumed on the third day, both Glendenen and Parker went on to complete centuries. Glendenen had

OXFORD UNIVERSITY v. DURHAM
at The Parks, Oxford, 14, 15, 16 April 1992
(Oxford University won the toss)

DURHAM	**1st innings**			**2nd innings**
J.D. Glendenen		b Gallian	117	
P.W.G. Parker		b Gallian	103	
D.M. Jones	not out		36	
P. Bainbridge	not out		24	
I. Smith				
+ C.W. Scott				
P.J. Berry				
G.K. Brown				
*D.A. Graveney				
S.M. McEwan				
J. Wood				
	Extras (2 b, 4 lb)		6	
	TOTAL (for 2 dec)		286	

Fall of wickets: 1–222, 2–235

Bowling	**O**	**M**	**R**	**W**
Jeh	20	4	74	0
Wood	12.3	0	39	0
Gallian	15	1	64	2
Davies	13.3	2	62	0
Anderson	5	0	25	0
Gupte	2	0	16	0

OXFORD UNIVERSITY	**1st innings**			**2nd innings**
R.R. Montgomerie	c Parker	b Bainbridge	17	
J.E.R. Gallian	c Scott	b Wood	53	
A. Storie	not out		23	
C.M. Gupte	not out		8	
*G.B.T. Lovell				
S.N. Warley				
D. Anderson				
+ R. Oliphant-Callum				
M. Jeh				
H.R. Davies				
B.S. Wood				
	Extras (4 nb)		4	
	TOTAL (for 2 wkts)		105	

Fall of wickets: 1–45, 2–89

Bowling	**O**	**M**	**R**	**W**
Wood	14	5	24	1
McEwan	11	4	26	0
Bainbridge	11	3	14	1
Smith	8	3	11	0
Berry	17	5	25	0
Graveney	4	1	5	0

Umpires: J.C. Balderstone & G. Sharp   **MATCH DRAWN**

the honour of recording Durham's first first-class century, just reaching the three-figure landmark before Parker did so for the forty-second time in his career. They shared an opening partnership of 222, and then allowed Dean Jones and Phil Bainbridge to ease their way to a fifty partnership before the declaration.

In the time remaining, Bainbridge took the first wicket with the help of a catch by Parker at slip, and John Wood saw Chris Scott take a catch behind for the second wicket. Oxford University had reached 105 for 2 from the 65 overs bowled when the match ended as a draw. It had been a useful if inconclusive exercise for Durham. The weather had been unkind, but they had the field for the first time as a first-class county in England and had done all that could be expected. More testing challenges were to come.

Durham v. Lancashire (Sunday League)

It was a quirk of the fixture list that all of Durham's first four matches as a first-class county should be played on the grounds of academic institutions. Whether this helped the learning process can only be a matter for speculation, but after The Parks the next stop was the Racecourse Ground, home of Durham University. The ground, on the banks of the Wear and with the cathedral towering imperiously from the city centre as a backdrop, was filled to its 6,000 capacity for the visit of Lancashire.

Appropriately enough, the first ball bowled in Durham's first Sunday League match was delivered by a graduate of Durham University. Paul Allott was, however, opening the bowling for Lancashire. Graeme Fowler was another Lancastrian who felt completely at home as a former Durham University cricketer, while Simon Hughes represented the University in the Durham side and was destined to bowl the last ball of the match.

Put in to bat, Durham openers Ian Botham and Wayne Larkins began cautiously against a side that had won four limited-overs trophies in the previous five years. They were in fact going at only three runs an over when Botham was out in the eleventh. This cleared the way for Dean Jones to join Larkins, and these two gradually raised the tempo. Larkins compiled a valuable half-century, but it was the Australian who stole the show. There were 2 6s in his first fifty, which came from just 45 balls. He hit 2 more 6s and 8 4s in all as he reached 114 in 103 minutes, before falling to the last ball of the innings.

He had been helped in the closing stages by Phil Bainbridge with 35 from the mere 23 balls he faced. Paul Parker was on hand for the final overs, contributing only 11 to a stand of 54 for the fourth wicket as Jones thrilled the crowd, delighted all those with Durham connections and destroyed Lancashire's attack. Durham's batsmen took 90 from the last 10 overs of the innings, while Jones recorded his second century in consecutive matches on the ground, having taken a ton off the Durham attack playing for Victoria at the end of 1991.

Lancashire were set the formidable scoring rate of 6.175 runs an over to win. Steve McEwan took 3 wickets and Simon Hughes 1 – that of his old university colleague Graeme Fowler – to have Lancashire struggling at 52 for 4. Speak and Watkinson staged a recovery and DeFreitas smote 33 from the 11 balls he faced. Hegg maintained the assault, and the target had been reduced to a perfectly feasible 19 runs to win from 2 overs.

With 7 balls to be bowled, only 10 were needed, and Allott went for the big hit off Simon Brown. Allott once clinched the League title for Lancashire with a similar blow which went for six. This one might have cleared the boundary as well had not Parker been at long-on to take the catch. The next ball, the first of the last over, was bowled by Hughes to last man Morrison. The New Zealander was an experienced cricketer, if limited in batting ability. He realised that the best chance his adopted county had of winning depended on his giving the strike to Hegg. He pushed the ball towards mid-on; Botham swooped and threw down the stumps with Hegg well short of his ground.

Sunday League cricket has been noted over the years for exciting finishes but, given the circumstances, there can have been few more dramatic finales than this. It might

DURHAM v. LANCASHIRE

at Durham University, 19 April 1992

Sunday League   **Lancashire won the toss**

DURHAM

I.T. Botham	st Hegg	b Allott	14
W. Larkins	c Austin	b Atherton	59
D.M. Jones	c Morrison	b DeFreitas	114
P. Bainbridge	c Fairbrother	b Morrison	35
F.W.G. Parker	not out		11
J.D. Glendenen			
+A.R. Fothergill			
S.M. McEwan			
S.P. Hughes			
+D.A. Graveney			
S.J.E. Brown			
	Extras (10 lb, 1 w, 2 nb)		13
	TOTAL (for 4 wkts)		246 (40 overs)

Fall of wickets: 1–33, 2–120, 3–192, 4–246

Bowling	O	M	R	W
Allott	8	0	30	1
Morrison	8	0	43	1
DeFreitas	8	0	53	1
Austin	7	0	46	0
Watkinson	5	0	34	0
Atherton	4	0	30	1

LANCASHIRE

G. Fowler		b Hughes	27
M.A. Atherton	c Hughes	b McEwan	11
G.D. Lloyd	c Brown	b McEwan	4
*N.H. Fairbrother	c Botham	b McEwan	2
N.J. Speak		b Hughes	58
M. Watkinson		b Botham	37
I.D. Austin	lbw	b Brown	27
P.A.J. DeFreitas		b Brown	33
+W.K. Hegg	run out		22
P.J.W. Allott	c Parker	b Brown	2
D.K. Morrison	not out		0
	Extras (1 b, 8 lb, 4 w, 1 nb)		14
	TOTAL		237 (39.1 overs)

Fall of wickets: 1–38, 2–48, 3–52, 4–52, 5–121, 6–168, 7–200, 8–213, 9–237

Bowling	O	M	R	W
McEwan	8	0	35	3
Brown	8	0	32	3
Hughes	7.1	0	31	2
Botham	8	0	57	1
Bainbridge	6	0	60	0
Graveney	2	0	13	0

Umpires: N.T. Plews & A.G.T. Whitehead   **DURHAM WON BY 9 RUNS** have been a trifle premature for the crowd to chant 'We're going to win the League!' but their reaction summed up the euphoria that was abroad. Dunelmians had seen their county play as a first-class county in a competitive match for the first time. They liked what they saw.

Durham v. Glamorgan
(Benson & Hedges Cup)

After drawing their first first-class game and winning their first Sunday League match, Durham lost their first outing in the Benson & Hedges Cup. They only just lost, Glamorgan getting home with 4 wickets but only four balls in hand, but still the match at the Racecourse Ground served to illustrate that it would not all be plain sailing for the newcomers. However, the fact that the early stages of this competition are played in qualifying groups meant that Durham were not out of the competition merely because of this first defeat.

David Graveney lost the toss for the third time in succession and Durham were once again put in to bat. It was not an auspicious start, for only 18 runs had been scored when Larkins, Glendenen and Jones were all back in the pavilion. When Geoff Cook had been talking about Ian Botham in a pre-season interview, he had remarked how the England all-rounder was never better than when presented with a challenge and that Durham would give him that challenge. With Durham at 18 for 3, Botham had his challenge.

Paul Parker and Phil Bainbridge helped him in partnerships of 62 and 44 as Botham held the innings together. Just as the Sunday League innings had been built around a century from Dean Jones, so this one hung on the fortunes of Botham. He was fourteen short of a deserved century himself when he fell to a catch by his old Somerset colleague Viv Richards. A score of 196 for 9 from their allotted 55

Appendix: The First Fixtures
DURHAM v. GLAMORGAN
at Durham University, 21 April 1992

Benson & Hedges Cup   **Glamorgan won the toss**

DURHAM
W. Larkins	c Croft	b Frost	0
J.D. Glendenen	c Richards	b Watkin	7
D.M. Jones	lbw	b Watkin	6
P.W.G. Parker		c & b Croft	22
I.T. Botham	c Richards	b Frost	86
P. Bainbridge	lbw	b Dale	22
+C.W. Scott	lbw	b Dale	3
*D.A. Graveney		b Frost	13
S.P. Hughes		b Frost	3
S.M. McEwan	not out		12
S.J.E. Brown	not out		4
	Extras (4 b, 7 lb, 7 w)		18

TOTAL (for 9 wkts)   196   (55 overs)

Fall of wickets: 1–1, 2–17, 3–18, 4–80, 5–124, 6–154, 7–166, 8–173, 9–176

Bowling	O	M	R	W
Watkin	11	6	20	2
Frost	11	4	26	4
Barwick	11	0	32	0
Croft	9	0	28	1
Dale	6	0	40	2
Cowdrey	7	0	39	0

GLAMORGAN
H. Morris	c Jones	b Brown	0
A. Dale	c Larkins	b Hughes	30
*M.P. Maynard	lbw	b Botham	1
I.V.A. Richards		c & b Botham	1
C.S. Cowdrey	c Graveney	b Hughes	78
P.A. Cottey	c Larkins	b Brown	38
R.D.B. Croft	not out		30
+C.P. Metson	not out		6
S.L. Watkin			
S.R. Barwick			
M. Frost			
	Extras (5 lb, 5 w, 3 nb)		13

TOTAL (for 6 wkts)   197   (54.2 overs)

Fall of wickets: 1–1, 2–3, 3–8, 4–52, 5–137, 6–183

Bowling	O	M	R	W
Brown	10	0	36	2
Botham	11	2	21	2
Hughes	10.2	2	32	2
Graveney	11	1	41	0
McEwan	7	0	32	0
Bainbridge	5	0	30	0

Umpires: J.D. Bond & B. Leadbeater   **GLAMORGAN WON BY 4 WICKETS** overs at least gave the Durham bowlers a total to defend, even if it was some thirty runs short of what they might have wanted.

When Glamorgan were 8 for 3, however, the Durham total appeared a long way off. This was especially the case as the three men out were all Test players: Morris, Maynard and the mighty Richards, who went to a spectacular caught-and-bowled by Botham. Dale steadied the innings for a time, but 52 for 4 left Durham in the favourite's position. A really powerful bowling attack might have been able to press home the advantage. Durham's attack had always been thought to have certain limitations and those shortcomings were now exposed by Chris Cowdrey, who had just been recruited by Glamorgan from Kent specifically for his expertise and experience of one-day cricket.

Cowdrey, helped by Cottey and Croft, steered Glamorgan towards their target with a defiant innings which totally justified his recruitment for just such a situation. His 78 was a fine, match-winning innings, but it was not enough to win him the individual award. That went to Ian Botham, ensuring that Durham did not end completely without reward for their efforts. It had always been known that to achieve success Durham would rely on their batsmen to score enough runs quickly so as to give their attack the opportunity to bowl at a side under pressure. On this occasion the batsmen had not scored heavily enough to create that pressure and, well though the bowlers performed, they were not quite able to deliver another victory.

Durham v. Leicestershire
(County Championship)

By Saturday 25 April 1992, Durham County Cricket Club had been involved in a first-class friendly match, the Sunday League and the Benson & Hedges Cup. County cricketers will tell you that of all the competitions in which they play, the one that means the most is the County Championship. This is the true test of a team's collective ability. Played over three or four days spread throughout the season, any weaknesses will be cruelly exposed, luck will even itself out, and only the strongest sides can hope to be in contention for the title at the end of the season.

Durham's players knew that, as a unit, they were not equipped to mount a serious challenge for the County Championship. Even so, they were determined to put up a spirited performance as they entered their first Championship match against Leicestershire at the Racecourse Ground. They did have genuine hopes of achieving some sort of success in one-day competitions, but confidence for those matches could be undermined by a poor showing elsewhere. Furthermore, Durham could achieve no sort of credibility as a first-class county without holding their own in the Championship.

Leicestershire arrived at the Durham University ground with an impressive opening to the season behind them. They had won their opening first-class match against Cambridge University by 133 runs after a double forfeiture of innings. They had had good wins over Gloucestershire and Sussex in the Benson & Hedges Cup and their one reverse of the season had been in the Sunday League at the hands of Middlesex. Their opening batsmen, Nigel Briers and Tim Boon, were in prolific form. David Graveney must have been delighted to win the toss and take first use of what was to prove a very slow pitch.

He was not quite so pleased when the Leicestershire attack made early, serious inroads into the Durham batting order. Wayne Larkins and Dean Jones were back in the pavilion for 5 and 2 respectively, with Durham on 18 for 2. None of the batsmen really came to terms with conditions except Paul Parker. He curtailed his attacking instincts to play a controlled innings of class, without which the total of 164 might well have been insufficient for the match to run its allotted course of four days. Leicestershire had moved to within 98 of that total by the end of the first day, but in the 24 overs bowled they had lost 2 wickets. Ian Botham caught and bowled the dangerous Briers before bowling former England batsman James Whitaker.

That second wicket had fallen with the score at 28, but it was to reach 101 before the third went down on Monday. In the meantime Durham were encouraged by another Sunday League success, this time by 8 runs. Durham scored 232 for 7, with Botham opening and scoring 67 and Glendenen (38) and Andy Fothergill (42 not out), the two 'Durham natives' in the side, sharing a stand of 58 for the sixth wicket. Leicestershire replied with 224 for 9 in their 40 overs, and Durham shared first place in the Sunday League with a one hundred per cent record.

Monday provided an altogether sterner proposition. Boon scored a century and Ben Smith was undefeated on 82 as Leicestershire ended the second day on 310 for 7, a lead of 146. Durham were already in a position where they were fighting to survive. They had taken two bowling bonus points to go with the one they had achieved while batting. They could not afford to allow Leicestershire to extend their lead very much further and still get away with a draw, unless the weather intervened.

The bowlers stuck to their task well, and on the Tuesday morning they managed to restrict Leicestershire's first-innings lead to 178 after Smith had completed his maiden first-class century. When Durham's second-innings score had reached 30 for 2, Jones and Parker again halted the slide towards ignominious defeat. They were forced to bat with extreme caution, but added 61 valuable runs before Jones was caught behind off the left-arm spin of Potter. Bainbridge soon followed, but Botham arrived to join Parker and by the close these two had taken Durham to a much more comfortable position. With a day to go, they had a lead of 5 runs with 6 second-innings wickets standing.

The final day illustrated to Durham folk almost all that is good in first-class county cricket. From a position where survival was the extent of Durham's ambition, Parker and, especially, Botham took on the Leicestershire attack with an intent that suggested a dramatic home win was not entirely out of the question. After receiving just 98 deliveries, Botham reached his century with 5 6s and 7 4s. Unfortunately for Durham he went for one big hit too many off the 105th ball he faced and was caught. He and Parker had put on 178 for the fifth wicket, so equalling the Durham record which had stood since 1955.

Botham's demise snuffed out any flickering hopes of a dramatic victory Durham might have quietly held. When Parker followed, having completed an equally valuable if less spectacular century, prospects of even salvaging a draw were dimmed. The tail folded under the pace of Millns; the Durham lead was 140, and Leicestershire had ample time to score those runs. Another thirty runs or so, along with

Durham

DURHAM v. LEICESTERSHIRE

at Durham University, 25, 27, 28, 29 April 1992

County Championship   **Durham won the toss**

DURHAM	1st innings			2nd innings		
W. Larkins	c Hepworth	b Mullally	5	lbw	b Mullally	9
J.D. Glendenen	c Mullally	b Wells	16	lbw	b Wells	18
D.M. Jones	c Briers	b Millns	2	c Whitticase	b Potter	32
P.W.G. Parker	lbw	b Wells	77		c & b Millns	117
P. Bainbridge	lbw	b Millns	19	c Briers	b Wells	9
I.T. Botham	c Whitticase	b Wells	12	c sub	b Millns	105
P.J. Berry	c Briers	b Potter	9	c Whitticase	b Millns	2
+C.W. Scott	c Whitticase	b Potter	0	lbw	b Millns	1
*D.A. Graveney	c Whitaker	b Mullally	12		b Wells	5
S.P. Hughes	not out		3	c sub	b Millns	1
S.J.E. Brown	c Whitticase	b Mullally	0	not out		2
	Extras 6 lb, 1 w, 2 nb)		9	Extras (2 b, 14 lb, 1 nb)		17
	TOTAL		164	**TOTAL**		318

Fall of wickets: 1–12, 2–18, 3–33, 4–82, 5–96, 6–132, 7–134, 8–156, 9–164

1–24, 2–30, 3–91, 4–112, 5–290, 6–292, 7–304, 8–315, 9–315

Bowling	O	M	R	W	O	M	R	W
Mullally	21.1	10	29	3	24	9	53	1
Millns	17	8	33	2	21.3	4	69	5
Wells	17	5	42	3	29	13	57	3
Parsons	14	1	31	0	12	3	28	0
Potter	13	3	23	2	26	10	50	1
Hepworth					8	0	45	0

LEICESTERSHIRE	1st innings			2nd innings		
*N.E. Briers		c & b Botham	10	c Parker	b Graveney	43
T.J. Boon	c Glendenen	b Berry	110	c Jones	b Botham	6
J.J. Whitaker		b Botham	2	c Hughes	b Berry	35
L. Potter	c Jones	b Graveney	31	not out		38
B.F. Smith	not out		100			
P.N. Hepworth	lbw	b Berry	8			
V.J. Wells	lbw	b Brown	42	not out		9
+P. Whitticase		b Hughes	11			
G.J. Parsons	c Scott	b Brown	10			
D.J. Millns		b Brown	6			
A.D. Mullally		b Hughes	1			
	Extras (8 lb, 3 nb)		11	Extras (2 b, 5 lb, 4 w)		11
	TOTAL		342	**TOTAL** (for 3 wkts)		142

Fall of wickets: 1–22, 2–28, 3–101, 4–197, 5–215, 6–287, 7–304, 8–327, 9–335

1–6, 2–63, 3–114

Bowling	O	M	R	W	O	M	R	W
Botham	25	10	51	2	5	2	7	1
Brown	26	2	80	3	3	0	10	0
Hughes	25	9	63	2	9	3	17	0
Graveney	28	6	80	1	12.2	2	37	1
Berry	26	7	60	2	12	4	44	1
Jones					7	0	20	0

Umpires: B. Dudleston & M.J. Harris **LEICESTERSHIRE WON BY 7 WICKETS** the shorter time that would then have been available, could have made the equation a little more interesting.

After an early success for Botham, the Leicestershire batting sensibly moved towards the target. Only 3 wickets had fallen and there were still 5 overs available when Durham's first match in the County Championship ended in defeat by 7 wickets.

It had been an eventful two weeks since that day in Oxford when those new sweaters and caps had been aired for the first time. The good ship Durham County Cricket Club had undergone her sea trials and, if she had found the waters just a little choppy, she was still afloat and making rather good headway against a strong current.

Index